# Shades of LIFE

MALCOLM NYGREN

# Shades of Life

## By Malcolm Nygren, S.T.D.

*Doxology Lane Press*
*3813 Fields South Court*
*Champaign, Illinois 61822*

*Printed by Martin Graphics & Printing Services*
*808 N. Country Fair Drive*
*Champaign, IL 61821*

# Acknowledgements

These pages were written over a period of years, and I am indebted to many people who contributed to making them possible.

Since our marriage my wife, Mimi, has read every column before it was published. Besides offering encouragement she has pointed out times when I did not write what I meant to say, and sometimes didn't write anything intelligible at all.

My daughters, Melinda Pierce and Nancy Nygren, have appeared anonymously in some of the columns and supportively in all of them. Each in her own way has made the bright shades of my life sparkle and made darker times bearable.

Joan Sensebrenner spent hours proofreading a large part of the manuscript. If there are any typographical errors in the book they must be from the parts she didn't read.

Jim Dey is the latest in a series of News-Gazette editors who, for their sins, were obliged to read every column and write a headline. Jim has often rescued me from grammatical confusion. For all this time the Gazette has honored my desire that the column appear on the editorial page with other opinionated columnists, and not in the religion ghetto.

Without George Grubb there would be no book. He planned and executed the actual printing as only a supportive friend would. Martin Graphics and Printing Services, and especially designer Jeremy Crawford, took a personal interest in the actual production of the book.

Liz Brunson and Kristie Cozad contributed their skills in photography. On a sunny summer afternoon they took the picture of me as seen on the cover of the book.

Becky Manley Pippert volunteered to write the Foreword. When I first saw it I was dismayed. I thought it was embarrassingly complimentary. Then I realized that many – if not most – ministers could be described in the same way. What she wrote about is what ministers do. That is why we love our profession.

The people of the First Presbyterian church of Champaign, Illinois gave me the vantage point from which to observe the many shades of life. A remarkably varied group, they were a good church, although not a famous one. It is exactly where I wanted to be and they were precisely the people I wanted to be with. I could have no better friends.

I am grateful for the faithful readers who have been the audience for these essays, either in newspapers, e-mail, or more recently in the blog: malcolmnygren. blogspot.com. Some I know personally, most I do not, but I've always had a better day when of them said, "I read your column."

Thank you, each of you.

# Foreword

Once when I was speaking in a remote part of the world I was asked by a local: "What tribe do you come from?" It was an astute question because he understood what Americans, who supremely value our individualism, conveniently tend to forget. We don't become who we are all by ourselves. All of us have been profoundly influenced by our tribe: our family, our traditions, our religious heritage, our community.

Isn't it fascinating for something so important – something that will shape our lives forever – that we have no say whatsoever in picking our tribe? God alone chooses our heritage.

One very important member of my God-given tribe has been Mal Nygren. He was the only pastor I ever knew growing up. From the time I was 4 years old when he baptized me, until I left for college at eighteen – Mal was my minister. When I returned to my home town in Champaign to go to graduate school at the University of Illinois – he was still there! When I joined the collegiate ministry organization of Inter Varsity Christian Fellowship it was Mal who performed the commissioning service in which I was sent and supported by First Presbyterian Church to minister in the wild, remote regions of the Pacific North West! Years later, living in Washington, D.C., I would bring my children Elizabeth and David to be baptized by him – just as he had baptized me. Upon reflection, Mal's influence in my life has been more that of tribal chief than mere minister!

I listened to Mal Nygren's sermons during the most formative years of my life. Several things impress me as I reflect on their influence. I can honestly say I never remember being bored – which is no small accomplishment coming from the perspective of a young person! His style of delivery was always lucid, logical, and thought provoking. Mal never thundered: he *invited* us to consider. He was wise and honest and described life as it was – but also told us how it *could be* with God's help. Though I didn't realize it at the time, my understanding of the nature of reality was being profoundly shaped hearing him preach. I learned that God is alive and real and we were created to know Him; that God is not only sovereign but He is good and can be trusted; and that people are flawed and need God desperately. Those ideas, which were so deeply embedded in his sermons, shaped me and my very understanding on the world. I have wondered over the years if Mal's great gift of preaching awakened and sparked in me the passion I have today to put God's deepest knowledge into words – whether in writing or speaking.

I also owe a great debt to Mal when, as a teenager, I began to question faith. As with most teens I began doubting what I believed. I read other religions and philosophies. Eventually I came to a point where I felt desperate to know if God was really there and if the claims of the Bible were true. One night as I lay in bed I cried out to God that, if He was there, I had to know one way or another. If God didn't exist and life was absurd, then I was willing to face that too, but I had to know.

Immediately a thought came to me with penetrating clarity: *call Mal Nygren.* I hadn't been to church in quite a while because of my spiritual wrestling. But the thought brought me such peace and calm that I was able to sleep.

It took me all the next day to get up my courage, but finally I called. I told him I was sure he was too busy to see me, but perhaps, oh maybe sometime in the next six months, I might drop in. On the contrary, he said, he would love to see today. I gulped and agreed to come after school.

Besides the fact that God [unbeknownst to me] had clearly put this idea in my head the night before, why would a teenager struggling with faith even consider going to talk to her pastor? Because having listened to Mal's sermons for most of my life, I knew he was intellectually honest. I knew no question or doubt of mine would unnerve him. And I knew he could be trusted to not push faith down my throat. That was definitely not his style.

Once inside his office I fired my questions. More than anything I was hoping he would say my spiritual crisis would pass and that it wasn't important. That he would say that all that was required to be a Christian was being kind and a good person. But he told me what I most dreaded to hear, that what Jesus said about his claims and demands was true. Then I said that if being a follower of Jesus meant that we actually come to know Christ personally, and surrender our entire lives to Him, it was clear to me that I was not a Christian nor had I ever been one. He said I was probably on target. His answers were wise, his manner was sensitive, but he was unswerving in his support of the gospel. The weight of God's truth and its implications left me feeling worse not better!

As I was leaving, he told me there was someone he wanted me to meet. Her name was Kewpie Renwick and she and her husband, Frank, were teaching an adult Sunday school class and he urged me to attend. I did, albeit, reluctantly. Yet it was in that class that I would eventually give my life to Jesus Christ - and my life would be forever changed.

Only later did I discover that Mal had called Mrs. Renwick asking her to

bilateral knee replace

redo 6/30/93
: 10-25-95 L

cataract surg
1995

thumbs : 1984

again in late 970
both eyes

Trip to Alaska 1992

Aug 29, 1991 - Trip to
Europe

Nov 02 - fell on garden
hip went out

...irts, sweatshirts, polo and long sleeved shirts des...
...viduals regarding their interest in purchasing a shir...

...il (nsgsa@yahoo.com) your requests.  Payment m...
...ceived.

| Navy/White | Small | Medium | Large | X-Large |
|---|---|---|---|---|
|  |  |  |  |  |
|  |  |  |  |  |
|  |  |  |  |  |
|  |  |  |  |  |
|  |  |  |  |  |
|  |  |  |  |  |

please take me into her already closed Sunday school class. *"Becky is right on the brink of becoming a Christian but she doesn't know it!"* Mal told her. Then Kewpie said to me, "Rev. Nygren has really been praying for you, Becky." I was thunder stuck – not once had it crossed my mind that Mal was praying for me during that crucial time in my life. When I thanked Mal many years later, for his deep influence in my life he responded with his characteristic modesty: "I was just doing my job!"

As we mature we slowly begin to see our mentors as real people. I had always been comforted by Mal's steady, rock-like stability and calm character. I enjoyed immensely his wry humor. I knew, even at a young age, that he was more than just intelligent. He was wise. But it was later I discovered that beneath his Swedish reserve lay a very deep reservoir of compassion and caring and profound loyalty.

It was also from the vantage point of adulthood, that I came to see that Mal had an unusual combination of humility and security. That is what made him a true leader. One characteristic of a true leader is not only delighting in the gifts of others but giving them the freedom to exercise their gifts freely. When Frank and Kewpie Renwick came to our church in the 1960's, Mal gave them free reign to minister. He didn't worry about whether they might steal his thunder nor did he try to control their gifts or influence. He delighted in the tremendous impact of their ministry. "God has a way of bringing angels in our midst," he said to me once "bringing just the right people at just the time we need them."

Likewise when I asked Mal, during my time of graduate study, if I could lead the Sunday School class for our High School youth, he gave me free reign to do whatever I wanted. How many pastors would give a young woman that kind of freedom and support? Soon I asked my dear friend, Beth [Goldhor] Domig to lead the Jr. High youth. I remember Mal's delight as our Youth Ministry grew and grew until we took up the first 7 rows at the front of the church every Sunday. "The students are actually writing notes on my sermons as I preach! Every minister's dream!" he said laughing.

Like all ministers Mal had to wear many hats: preacher, counselor, administrator, manager. How God used him to build First Presbyterian church during his 40 year tenure is a beautiful story in itself. But Mal has worn another hat that is often unrecognized. The columns you are about to read are written less from his pastoral role and more from his role as an astute evangelist. His columns were written for the broadest possible audience: from skeptic to seeker to believer. Through these nuggets of wisdom he was challenging his readers to made sense out of life – to not live an unexamined life - to see the connections between themselves and God. His desire was to create in his readers a curiosity and hunger for meaning that might one day cause them to be open to investigating Christ. But all of his columns were written against the unspoken backdrop of this one great truth -which I will let Mal say in his own words: "Life fits together only if one thing is true: that Jesus died for our sins and lives for our forgiveness."

Several years ago I saw the film *Mr. Holland's Opus*. At the end of the film there is a poignant scene in which Mr. Holland's former students gather to express their gratitude for Mr. Holland's influence in their lives. I only vaguely remember the speech in the film. But let's imagine that all of the people Mal has touched and influenced over the years - from his early days as a young pastor to his retirement at First Presbyterian - to his beloved family – and to all those who have been helped by his columns - have gathered together, with him, in our beautiful sanctuary. This is what I would say because I believe it represents what all of us would want to say to Mal in our gratitude for his influence in our lives:

"Mal Nygren had a profound influence on my life, and I know on your lives as well. Over the years he had many offers to leave and pastor elsewhere. But he didn't. Instead he chose to stay in one town and committed himself to one congregation. That was not the career path to ensure fame and wealth. Because the truth is, Mal Nygren isn't rich and he isn't famous, at least not outside of our little town.

So it might be easy for him to think that the sphere of his influence was limited. And he would be wrong, because I think that he's achieved a success and influence far beyond riches and fame.

Look around you, Mal. There is not a life in this room that you have not touched, and each one of us has learned to love God more dearly and follow him more faithfully, because of you.

*We* are your sermon, Mal. We are the living text of your sermons that you prepared and labored over for 40 years. And we are the living fruit of your faithful prayers for us during all of your life – a fruit that will last for eternity. We could never adequately express our thanks to you. But what heartens us is the knowledge that one day God will."

**Rebecca Manley Pippert**
**Louisville, KY**
**April 23, 2007**

# Biographical Note

Malcolm Nygren was an unusual minister. He served only one church -- in Champaign, Illinois -- but stayed there for 39 years. His congregation was made up of nearly equal numbers of faculty of the University of Illinois and townspeople. During World War II he was in the infantry, serving in Europe. When the war ended he studied to be a Presbyterian minister. He never stopped being a student. With degrees from Hanover College (B.S.) McCormich Theological Seminary (M.Div} and San Francisco Theological Seminary (S.T.D.), he later studied at Oxford University's Mansfield College, the International Center in Rome, and the Orthodox Academy on Crete. His weekly newspaper column has appeared on the editorial page of the Champaign-Urbana News Gazetter for many years.

# Love, Betrayal, Jealousy, and Despair

This is a story about love, betrayal, jealousy and despair. It is not a pretty tale. Tango was a Blue and Gold Macaw, an elegant bird, proud of his plumage. He lived on a boat with Bill. Tango and Bill laughed and sang and played games together. In one of their favorite games Tango would call "Stick 'em up!" and Bill would throw his hands in the air and they would both laugh and laugh.

Then Bill met The Woman. After a while The Woman came to live on the boat. The Woman was very tidy (Bill wasn't) and she didn't like Tango because sometimes his feathers fell out. She also didn't like for Bill to laugh with Tango instead of paying attention to her.

"That bird belongs in a zoo," The Woman said. "He would be a lot happier there." What she meant was that she would be a lot happier if Tango were anywhere except on the boat. But in the end Bill took Tango to a little zoo on Sanibel Island, where there were macaws and cockatoos and parrots and even a few monkeys.

Tango might have been happy on a boat, with someone else who liked to play games. He wasn't happy in the zoo. He wasn't used to living in a cage out of doors, to having strangers come and stare at him, to being with other birds that had never lived with people. He wasn't happy without Bill.

Tango knew he wasn't loved any more and he felt unlovable. He began to pull at the beautiful feathers on his chest. Soon he had plucked them all out, and he was as unlovely as he felt. Now Tango looks like a broiler chicken in the supermarket. Still, when someone comes near, he still says, "Stick 'em up!" in a small, sad voice. Nobody laughs.

How do you explain to a bird that to be unloved doesn't mean you're unlovable? How do you tell Tango that God sees the sparrows fall and loves a macaw that is caged in a zoo? It is hard enough for people to know that, and many of us need to know it.

# The Terrible Freedom of Faith

Peace and good will are in short supply this year, as they are every year. Dictators are pressing to seize the nuclear swords that can destroy civilization. Crazed fanatics are slaughtering their neighbors in African streets and Bagdad slums. Cults teach children to hate before they learn to write. Suicidal murders are honored. Innocents have nowhere to hide.

Sometimes peace and good will seem so close. After the First World War statesmen announced that the killing fields of Flanders had made the world safe for democracy. It didn't. When Hitler was driven to the bunker where he died and Mussolini's corpse strung up in a village square the world hoped for peace at last. They were evil personified, and evil had been overcome.

We failed to understand something as old as Cain and Abel. There is always another Hitler, lusting for power, plotting to teach hatred and destroy peace.

Castro is sick and impotent and Saddam is in the dock, and peace has not come. Their successors are in the wings, slashing at one another until one has claimed the throne. There will always be another Hitler. What others see as temptation they see as opportunity.

It is because of what we are. Some of us are saints, delighting in sacrificing for others. Some of us are evil, inflicting suffering without compunction. Most of us wander in between, sometimes loving, occasionally hurtful, and mostly neither. We all have this terrible freedom, without which there would be no Hitler – and no Mother Theresa.

This is both the blessing and the curse of being human. We are animals, but we are more than animals. We are accountable for what we do, only a little lower than the angels. We are free to soar, and so we must be free to do terrible harm.

There will always be another Hitler. There will always be another Mother Theresa. We are sent to choose our way through this troubled, troubling world. There will be no final victory of our making. We can only win our personal victory, by choosing which side we are on, by rescuing the victims within our reach.

The final victory belongs to God.

# What God Won't Do

In Mark Twain's novel *A Connecticut Yankee in King Art hur's Court* the Yankee wanted to destroy the credibility of the wizard Merlin. He gave Merlin the job of forecasting the weather. Nobody would believe a thing he said after a few weeks at that job.

Meteorologists have more status today, but it is still an uncertain profession. They've learned to give us probabilities, not certainties. Instead of "rain tomorrow" they tell us there is a "ninety percent chance of rain", which allows for the wayward ways of wind and clouds.

When a famously successful investor was asked what the stock market would do next year he predicted that it would fluctuate. His reputation wasn't damaged by that call. Religious leaders are wise not to predict the end of the world on a date that is certain. In the 19th century that was done on several occasions. Each time it left the seer with a lot of explaining to do.

In the last decades of the 20th century predicting was a fad. A new kind of expert appeared: the futurologist. Some futurologists were optimistic, some were pessimistic. None of them were reliably accurate.

Predicting the future is a risky enterprise. That's why I don't find much comfort in the slogan that "God is in charge." I can easily believe that God can do anything. That's the definition of God. What I don't know is what God will choose to do.

I can accept the notion that whatever happens will in the end prove to be all right, and that at some future time we will see the good in it. What I don't know is whether that knowledge will come in this world or the next, and that makes an enormous difference.

I can however know what God will not choose to do. God will not take away from us our terrible freedom to choose selflessness or selfishness, to live for others or for our desires alone. God will not bribe us with instant rewards or frighten us with immediate dangers.

We can't know what the future will bring to the world. We still have to choose what we will bring to the future.

# Bigger, Faster, Louder

I have never uttered the magical phrase, "Super-size it!" I get in enough trouble with normal portions. What this country needs is smaller servings of better food. What we are getting is thicker burgers. I would be a customer of any restaurant that would let you say, "Miniaturize it!"

It won't be an easy sell. We are committed to the belief that bigger is better and enormous is best of all. We salivate at the sight of a sign that says, "All you can eat!"

We believe that popularity is the same as quality. We buy the books that have the biggest sales and listen to the music that sells out the biggest arenas. We go to movies that have mega-million dollar budgets and a cast the size of a small republic. Everything is amplified. If a little music is good, making it loud enough to stun a cockroach must be really, really good.

The Little Brown Church in the Wildwood is gone. It has been replaced by the megachurch just off the freeway. Everything is getting bigger and faster and louder. We are deafened by the rush and noise. We are overwhelmed by the sheer size of things.

A psalmist quoted the Almighty as saying, "Be still, and know that I am God." A prophet said that God spoke "in a still, small voice." That was in a different age, when things moved more slowly and life was quieter and smaller. Hardly anyone is still today, and small voices are usually drowned out.

We must make our own quiet and calm in the midst of the noisy frenzy. The loudest voice may get the most attention, but the quiet determination of the few will do more good. Faith isn't something we shout into existence. It whispers in our ear and lays a gentle hand on our shoulder.

Faith comes quietly and lasts long. In the tumults and terrors of life it is like a song heard softly in the distance. It is not the loudest voice or the biggest sound, but it is the most persistent. In difficult times it is the only song that gives us hope. All the rest is just noise.

# We Have Looked on the Worm

There's something worse than finding a worm in an apple you're eating. It's finding half a worm.

Unfortunately there are a lot of worms we don't worry about until after we bite the apple. Americans have known about terrorism for a long time. It was something that happened to strangers in distant places. It wasn't until it happened in our homeland to people like us that we took the half worm seriously.

Now that we have looked on the worm we are different people. Our values are different. We are more serious and less likely to take important things for granted. We don't have to apologize for loving our country. We care more about things that neither moth nor rust nor terrorist's bombs can corrupt.

That's the good news, but it isn't the only news. Wars, even shadowy wars against terror, don't make people better. They magnify our character. They enlarge the best and the worst in us.

There is no greater love than this: to lay down your life for another. We don't have many chances to do that in peacetime. It happens often in a war. There is no greater selfishness than to desert friends in danger or brutalize the helpless. Those things happen, too.

Noble causes don't make noble people. The American Civil War was a noble cause that ended slavery in this country. It also resulted in the creation of some very large fortunes for those willing to profit from the war.

The Viet Nam War was the source of more moral controversy than any event in American history. Not all the soldiers were heroes. Not all the objectors had a conscience. It was never clear who were heroes and who were not. The passage of time has only deepened the confusion.

A great deal has changed, but not everything. The same terrible times that make heroes create cowards, traitors, and profiteers. Danger does not make us better. It makes us decide.

God gave us this terrible freedom. We have looked upon the worm. We must choose now what we will do about it. That was true before terrorism came to America, but it matters more now.

# Cut-rate Commitment

My second cousin Susanne Gunnarrson won a gold medal in the Olympic Games. Well, actually she's my second cousin's daughter, a second cousin once removed. She's removed across an ocean as well. She lives in Sweden, and I've never met her.

That's not exactly a close brush with fame, but it made the Games more interesting to me and my family. Instead of an impersonal news event the Olympics were a personal adventure. We weren't just interested spectators. We were involved.

There are different levels of involvement, and this was involvement at a pretty low level. It cost me nothing, took no more time than I wanted to give it, and although I wanted my cousin to win it wouldn't have cost a night's sleep if she didn't. It didn't change anything in my life. It was bargain basement involvement.

That's always been the most popular way to be involved, but it is particularly favored now. Relationship without commitment is the name of this low cost game. We shop for the cheapest bargain in relationships we can find.

The commitment between employers or employees is good only until the next downsizing or the next contract negotiations, whichever comes first. There are no longer baseball teams. There is only a group of migrant players, who happen to have chased the dollars to this city for this year.

There are relationships instead of marriages. They cost less. Even marriages sometimes begin with a minimal commitment and end with the maximum rancor. The marriage hasn't gone bad. It was always bad. It didn't cost enough.

We get what we pay for. If we pay a cheap price we get cheap goods. If we make the smallest possible commitment we will enjoy the smallest possible happiness.

The Bible exhorts us to love God with all our heart and mind and soul, and to love our neighbor as ourselves. That's a real commitment. That's a faith that changes everything we are and do, from the way we care for our family to the way we care about strangers on the street.

There's nothing cheap about that but it's worth the price. Anything less is too cheap.

# Small Town Morals

I like small towns. Philo may not be the center of the universe but it's a pleasant place. There's nothing imposing about the town square in Oakland, but it's peaceful. Walking around a small town, where there isn't a lot of traffic and nobody crowds you off the sidewalk, is good for tattered nerves.

The people are nice. Small town people aren't any better than anybody else. They just know more about each other. Merchants have to sell to the same people year after year. This is a powerful incentive to fair dealing and good service. The alternative is moving frequently. Very frequently. Word gets around fast in a small town.

It doesn't take a lot of character to behave well in a small town. Everybody is watching. There are scandals in small towns, but they are noticed, discussed, disapproved, and remembered forever. Staying on the strait and narrow path is as much a matter of good sense as it is of good morals.

Good morals and good sense are never far apart. The Ten Commandments aren't the mindless regulations of a heavenly bureaucracy. They are good sense. They point people to a safe and happy life, "so that it may go well with them and with their children forever." They are ways to avoid hurting others and destroying ourselves.

When we say someone has no morals we might as well say they have no sense. They are not rational. At the bottom there is not a thinking person. There is only appetite: appetite for money or food or sex or power or for all of them. Duty and responsibility count for nothing. Nothing counts but appetite.

Immorality can be clever but not wise. It thinks short term. It looks to the next meal, the next successful lie, the next conquest. It can be sated but never satisfied. It isn't sensible and it doesn't bring happiness. It hardens sensitivity and destroys kindness.

It's not impossible to be that dumb in a small town, but it's a little harder. Your neighbors will notice and tell you about it. They'll tell everyone else about it too.

# Contentment and Happiness

"I am content," a friend said to me several months ago. "That's not the same as happy, but in some ways it's better."

She was a sensible lady. Happiness is a rare state. It is the day when our steps are lighter than air, when all the colors are rich and bright, when we are glad to be alive.

The difference between happiness and contentment is that happiness comes from outside and contentment comes from within us. We are happy when someone wonderful tells us they will marry us, or we have won the lottery, or the gold medal of victory is hung around our shoulders.

We are contented when, like the poet Browning, we know that "God's in his heaven" and "all's right with the world." Contentment is not the result of what happens to us. Contentment is because of who we are.

When we are most happy we are most vulnerable. Even small annoyances can break the joyful spell. Dinner time telemarketers have much to answer for. Forces we don't control can snatch away our happiness in a moment's time. A sickness we never expected or a death that comes too early can change everything. A dream that is lost can turn off the sunlight. Troubles large and small lie in wait for us, and all can interrupt our happiness. We are at the mercy not only of our own safety, but the safety of those we love.

Contentment is not so fragile. When we are happy it is because we think that life could not be better. When we are content we know that it could be a lot worse. Contented people remember their happiest days with pleasure. Happy people don't get the same satisfaction from remembering contentment. Most of us are contented more often than we are happy.

We usually pray for happiness, in one form or another. We pray for something good to happen to us. Sometimes it does. At other times that prayer is answered with the gift of contentment. What happens is soon forgotten. Who we become lasts forever. God is more interested in how we are changed by life than in what we get from it.

# One Mistake is All You Are Allowed

People don't like snakes very much. Most snakes are harmless, but some are deadly. We aren't quite sure which ones those are. But that isn't the only problem. Even harmless snakes aren't cuddly like kittens. You don't want to curl up with a good book and hold a serpent in your lap.

Venomous cobras or giant pythons are feared but not respected. Lions are dangerous too, but they aren't despised like snakes. Lions are respected. A British king was called Richard the Lion-hearted. Richard would have been pretty upset if anyone called him Richard the Snake-hearted.

In some countries dangerous snakes are a hazard of daily life. They lurk in the grass and shrubs and may strike at any time. That isn't true here. There aren't many snakes where we live, and hardly any that are deadly. I have never known anyone who was bitten by a venomous snake or squeezed by a constrictor. I don't expect to. That doesn't make people like snakes any better.

This isn't fair to snakes. They are the victims of species profiling. Because some snakes are murderous all snakes are feared. Even harmless little grass snakes are unwelcome in our gardens. Everybody knows that profiling is wrong.

Like most things that everybody knows, this is only partly true. On the coral islands of the Caribbean only some of the brightly colored snakes are venomous. Still, tourists are well advised to avoid them all. One mistake is all you are allowed.

In the peaceful world where we once lived suspicion or distrust was unwarranted. Everyone was innocent until they were proved guilty. We don't live in that world any more. Guilt may be indisputable only in the shadow of a mushroom cloud. One mistake will be too many.

This isn't the world we wanted to live in. We would like to have the old security back. We can't bring it back. The question is not whether we will live in a trusting, peaceful world or one that is very dangerous. We don't have the luxury of such a pleasant choice. There are people who want to kill us.

These are serious times. The serious question is whether we will live or die.

# The Problem with Believing

I'm a Chicago Bears fan but not a very serious one. I know where my loyalties lie but I don't expect everyone to agree. If someone is fanatically attached to the Green Bay Packers that's all right.

Some of my best friends are Packer fans. Besides, it's not a matter of life or death.

For people who wear their religion like an NFL tee shirt it seems easy to solve the problem of religious conflict. To them all religions are equal, all basically alike. Choosing one or the other or none isn't an important decision.

But for many people their faith is a matter of life or death. It defines who they are and how they see the world. They can't imagine life without it. They know others don't share their faith, but they see that lack as a very serious matter. At best they want to live for their faith. They may risk dying for it. Sadly, sometimes they are willing to kill for their faith.

This behavior is completely unintelligible to people who don't have much faith of any kind. For people who are deeply committed to their own faith however, it is a serious question. In a democratic, diverse society it is a question faced by Christians, Jews, Muslims, Buddhists and every other faith that flocks to America. How do we stay true to our faith when our neighbors don't share it?

How can faith be deep and sincere without being fanatical? How can neighbors respect one another when each rejects the most important commitments of the other? How do you love your neighbor as yourself when your neighbor isn't like you?

These are very difficult questions. We have at least made a beginning when we honestly recognize that they are serious questions. We must not be satisfied with easy evasions. These questions are, like faith itself, questions of life and death.

It doesn't help to say that all religions are alike. That is nonsense. They are very different. We must each learn to live with the differences in ways that respect the faith of others without abandoning our own. We must express the best in our own faith, not the worst.

# Some People are Prettier than They Look

A dead raccoon lay beside the road, the victim of a passing truck. I felt a little sad when I saw it. I never feel that way when I see a dead opossum, but a raccoon is a pretty animal and an opossum is not. A coon's dainty paws and bandit face and magnificent tail touch my heart. An opossum, which looks like a big rat on a bad hair day, does not. Looks aren't everything, but they matter all the same.

Looks matter with people too, but it is a little more complicated than that. It's said that beauty is in the eye of the beholder, but that is only partly true. It is also in the character of the beheld.

Abraham Lincoln wasn't the Hollywood ideal of masculine charm, yet we look on his face with satisfaction. We know who he was and what he did, and we are reassured by what we know. No blow-dried politician has such charm.

One December I looked out of my office window and saw an elderly couple I knew. They held hands and looked at one another with unfeigned affection. He clearly saw a beautiful woman, and she saw a handsome man. That wasn't because they had an unusual capacity for seeing beauty. It was because each knew enough about the other to see the essential beauty in them.

That's why I am happy about the current Miss America, Erica Harold. I have no idea how she looks in a swim suit. I do know that she has overcome rejection and hurt with grace, that she has developed her talents to their utmost, and that she makes her parents proud. That is beautiful.

We all know people who seem more beautiful than they appear. No photograph ever captures them. Their likeness is never more than that, emptied of the joy that is their nature. You can't put enthusiasm or kindness on a piece of paper.

Isaiah wrote something strange. He said "How beautiful on the mountains are the feet of the messenger who announces peace." Can feet be beautiful? Of course they can. It's not a matter of admiring toes, but of knowing where they walked.

# Faith Is Powerful and Dangerous

I was once invited to see the pictures an agriculture professor had taken on a trip to Switzerland. I like mountain scenery, so I was disappointed to find that he had taken no pictures of mountains. What he showed me were fields of corn, wheat and oats.

I thought this was strange until I noticed that when I travel I bring back a lot of pictures of churches. A visitor from another planet would believe that I think churches are important. The visitor would be right.

Swiss farms and English churches are both important. We can't live without eating. We don't need to live without praying.

One of the heresies of this century is the notion that religion should be separated from the rest of life. It is the belief that faith must concern itself only with religious questions. Faith must be isolated from politics, business, and diplomacy. The laws we pass and the votes we cast must never be influenced by religion, either ours or those of a candidate.

This relegates faith to the status of a hobby. It is something we do because we want to do it. It has no significance for the larger questions of life. This is quite agreeable to people who have no faith or wear their faith lightly. They can't understand people who put faith at the center of their life.

This creates a dilemma. All important questions are religious questions. That doesn't make it any more likely that all religious answers will be good answers. Some may be very bad indeed.

In history we have seen often that faith is powerful and dangerous. Slavery was supported by pious invocations of Scripture. The Taliban in Afghanistan did harsh things in the name of God. The pseudo-religion of Marxism excused slaughters and despotism. The faithful followers of these faiths were fanatically devoted and certain that what they did was right.

Faith is strong medicine. It isn't harmless. Faith can heal deep wounds or cause great evil. The failures of faith are not a reason to shut faith out of our life. Because faith is powerful we need to take very seriously what we believe and what we condone.

# Angels Don't Campaign to be Elected

I like advertising. Some television commercials and print ads are funny, some tell us things we want to know, some are even interesting. They aren't usually annoying. If you want to sell someone a cell phone, a car, or a detergent you try very hard not to annoy the customer. At campaign time the rules are tossed out. It is okay to annoy people.

We will all be glad when this election is over. More money is being spent on advertising than ever before. Most of that money is used to annoy voters. Candidates want us to dislike and distrust their opponents. They make us dislike elections and distrust the people who are elected.

I particularly dislike the ads touting someone who says he or she will fight for me in Washington or Springfield. I don't want anyone to fight for me. I'm not mad at anyone and I don't feel threatened by the state or federal governments. The idea of someone snarling and growling to snatch more from the governmental money trough for me is repellant. The implication of these ads is that I am greedy. I don't like to be told that.

We see two pictures of every candidate: the one invented by their hired spin doctors, and the one imagined by their opponent's spin doctors. They are either valiant fighters for "the little man" or blind servants of "special interests." There don't seem to be any ordinary people running on either side.

The thing we must remember during an election is that despite their claims no candidate is supernaturally pure. All have sinned and fallen short of whatever glory they claim. We do not have the luxury of voting for angels. We have to make do with humans who are no better than we are. We can only hope that they aren't a lot worse. For the most part, people elect people like themselves and get the government they deserve.

Some day someone will produce a campaign commercial that is funny. It won't be sarcastic or mean spirited. It will be the work of a normal person who can laugh at their own foibles. That person, of course, will not be elected.

# The Heavenly Gift of Sweet Corn

Another sweet corn season is nearly over. It's sad to know that it will be almost a year before we will taste the succulent kernels again.

There will still be sweet corn, of course. You can get sweet corn in the winter in Florida, but it isn't the same. Growing corn in Florida is like making wine in Illinois. It can be done, but there is no good reason why it should.

Corn needs the rich Midwestern soil and the hot Midwestern sun. Anything else produces a parody of sweet corn, a grain that looks the same but tastes disappointingly different.

Sweet corn is the most perishable of crops. It begins to lose its flavor the moment the ear is parted from the stalk. Every year Dick Burwash gives me the best corn I eat. Dick is a farmer who knows corn. He has it picked in the morning and dropped in a tank of ice water. In the afternoon it's cooked in the husk over a charcoal fire. Even fastidious people strip off the husk, slather the corn with butter, dash it with salt, and gnaw on the ears like starving peasants.

An ancient Hebrew prayer says, "Blessed are you O God, King of the Universe, who brings forth bread from the earth." Not only bread but sweet corn and the butter and salt that make it savory. We have many reasons to be thankful, and the food we enjoyed this summer is one of the most basic.

Everything has its season and every season ends. That's true of sweet corn and the careers of Olympic athletes. College ends, a summer vacation ends, a good movie ends. Children grow up and both the joys and troubles of parenthood end,

When blessings end we can either be sad at their loss or be grateful that we enjoyed them. Either is possible, but only one extends our happiness. If we think about what we no longer have the pleasure is marred by sorrow. If we rejoice when we remember what we have had we still enjoy it.

Blessed are you, O God. We enjoyed it, and we are glad it was ours to enjoy.

# The Tuition is High at the School of Experience

The two evergreens that hide our gas meter died. One was replaced last summer but the other wasn't. This spring I carefully measured the tree that was planted last year. That was so I could buy another exactly the same height.

That wasn't a good idea. The trees matched for a few weeks. Then the older tree grew rapidly and the new one didn't grow at all. Instead of identical twins I have an Arnold Schwarzenegger tree and a Danny De Vito tree. The shock of transplanting stunted the growth of the new tree. The other one had a year to recover and grow normally.

I've learned something from this experience, but it won't do me much good. I'll probably never have this problem again. Experience is a good teacher but there are two things wrong with it. Many of the problems we face we have never experienced before, and many of the experiences that taught us we'll never have again.

That's true of being a parent. Parents learn many things from the first child. They learn one thing from the next: that child is nothing like the first. By the time they have learned a lot they are grandparents. Grandparents only need to know two things: first, you can always send them home, and second, if they do something wrong it isn't your fault.

Marriage is something we learn by experience, but it's expensive learning. Sometimes the marriage is ruined before the lesson is learned. Long marriages are good when both have learned what makes the other happy and what makes them unhappy. Nobody forgets their anniversary twice, but it would be better not to forget it once. You learn that by experience, but only if you want to.

Commitment is more important than experience. Parents who are committed to love their children and couples who are committed to love one another will learn what they need to know. Without commitment nothing is learned. There is no reason to learn.

I'm not committed to planting trees. I hope I never plant another. Making the right commitments is more important than having the right experiences.

# Getting Better at Doing Worse

The postal service has taken to playfully sticking bar codes on postcards. There are two. One defaces the picture side of the card. The other they put on the message part, usually so that it covers the signature. This allows us to play guessing games like "Where in the World is Carmen Santiago" or "Who the Heck is in San Diego?"

Sometimes the handwriting is recognizable, but since postcards are often hastily written on a bus or after a ten hour flight it may not be their usual Spenserian script. The message offers clues, but they can be puzzling. Postcard writers usually only tell you that this is a beautiful place and they're having a great time except for a head cold and a slight gastrointestinal problem.

The sticker is reasonably easy to peel off. That's good. Usually it takes part of the card with it. That's bad. There's a white blob on the picture and you still don't know who sent the card. It's hardly worth the postage to send someone a defaced photo and an anonymous message.

Almost certainly those bar codes are there for a sorting machine of some kind. A scanner peers at them and sends the cards off in the right direction. This demonstrates a trend in technology. We are getting better and better at doing things that become less and less worth doing.

We travel faster and farther to do things that are increasingly trivial. We fax documents across continents and oceans without improving the quality of what we communicate. The invention of e-mail was closely followed by the invention of junk e-mail. The scam artists are hot on the heels of the technology wizards.

The optimistic claim that the Information Age would bring the world closer together and usher in the Age of Peace is a false hope. Better communication spreads lies and vilification as quickly as kindness and truth.

The demons that haunt our age are not a problem of communication. They are a moral problem, and there is no technology fix for that. As Jesus once said of a different demon, "This kind can come out only through prayer."

# Life Isn't Happy Because of What We Get

E-mail is a growing fad, the CB radio of the 90's. You can have a letter delivered in minutes instead of days and save money every time you do it. You don't need a state of the art computer to use it. A second hand machine with no resale value will do.

You can also get a lot of junk mail. Junk e-mail is multiplying on the Internet like maggots on yesterday's road kill.

Some of it offers health products of untested worth. Some are offers to make you rich in six months – less, if you answer today. The clear winner for crassness is the person who offers to sell you software so you can flood the Internet with messages to ten thousand strangers at once, just as he is doing.

Like most things in America this has led to lawsuits. The courts are wrestling with a question: can an online service refuse to deliver junk e-mail if its customers don't want it? The sender has a right to free speech. Does the recipient have a right to not listen?

There are sad lands where nobody has any rights and everybody has duties. In our country everybody has rights but we can't sort out whose rights come first. This doesn't leave much time to think about anyone's duty.

We don't talk about duty much. Responsibility is a softer word, but that isn't too popular either. It's easy to understand why. Rights are something you get. Duty is something you give. Getting is always more popular than giving.

People obsessed with getting never get enough. Not enough power, not enough money, not even enough rights. Rights are good. So are power and money. People without rights are miserable, and so are those who are powerless and poor. But having these things doesn't satisfy us. We never get all we want, so we don't really enjoy what we have.

Responsibility is satisfying. It is satisfying to keep the vows of marriage, to do the duties of parents, to fulfill the promises of faith. We are content. It isn't what we get that makes life happy. It's what we give.

# Happiness, Without Additives

Our house is being painted. That means I have to open all the windows before the paint dries. If I don't my house will be hermetically sealed – forever.

With air conditioning, thermostatically controlled heat, electronic air filters and a humidifier I don't really need to open any windows. It is just that on a nice day I like unprocessed air, without any additives. There are few enough days in the year when the air is fresh and pleasant, when it's not hot or humid or cold. I don't want to miss any part of those days.

Fresh air on a fall day is a simple pleasure. There are others: the call of doves in the early morning, the taste of cold water on a hot day, the sun painting the western skies at evening. They are neither sophisticated nor naïve. Shakespeare could enjoy them as much as we, the stable boy as much as Shakespeare. Anyone can afford them, anyone can appreciate them.

Most of our entertainment is manufactured. It is produced by professionals and shown to us by technicians. It is aimed at a particular market, a specific level of intelligence and culture. Some people are ecstatic about it, others detest it. Some can afford it, others do without. It is not universally available or enjoyed.

That's all right. There are some television shows I don't like to miss and some music I like to hear. They're not everyone's choice, but they're mine and I would be poorer without them.

But these are not the only pleasures in life. If my television set goes blank, all the theaters close, and the artificial turf in the stadium turns to crabgrass my life will not be empty. My happiness does not depend on national rankings or points on the Nielsen scale.

In fact happiness doesn't even depend on fresh air, cold water, and sunsets. It depends on the God who gives us universal gifts and created us able to enjoy them. Happiness comes from knowing who we are, and knowing who made us the way we are.

# My Fifteen Minutes of Fame

Most people rake the leaves in their yard in the fall. We've been raking leaves in our living room all summer. Some friends gave us a small tree as a housewarming present more than twenty years ago. It's now in a pot too big to move without a forklift.

It is also apparently dying. Leaves are falling every day. Soon I'll have a decision to make. Either I call in a forester to remove a dead stump from my living room or I learn to appreciate bare branches as an artistic statement.

Presenting a dead tree as a work of art isn't impossible. Stranger things have been hailed as works of genius. A dead tree that was somehow pornographic would be a sure winner. I'm not sure how to do that. Only that one technical problem separates me from my fifteen minutes of fame.

It's true that some works of art are hard to understand and some are easy. It only takes a few minutes and not much thinking to get all there is to get out of a comic strip. Anyone can understand it because there isn't much to understand.

You can look at a Norman Rockwell illustration a little longer and find things worth your time. It doesn't take much preparation though. Everything you see is from the world you know and you recognize it easily.

Beyond that is the world of art and music and performance that requires skill by the audience as well as the artist. As it becomes loftier more and more is experienced by fewer and fewer people. A perfect work of art would be one in which all of life could be experienced, but only by one person.

Art walks a line between everybody understanding a little and a few people understanding a lot. Even Shakespeare had to sell enough tickets to keep the Globe Theater running. If he hadn't we wouldn't remember him.

That's the problem religion always faces. What's the goal? Pack in the crowds by saying very little in an interesting way, or say a lot to small audiences?

Does anybody want a large dead potted tree?

# Thank God the World Isn't Fair

I'm not a dedicated gardener. In fact, I'm hardly a gardener at all. But sometimes I get better results than I deserve.

This summer has been full of distractions. My only attempt at growing flowers was one afternoon in the Spring when I bought some plants and put them in the ground. Since then I haven't even looked at the yard. No watering, no fertilizer, no weeding.

I was surprised when I glanced out the kitchen window to see a brilliant display of color along the edge of the porch. The dahlias I planted several months ago are flourishing. There are no weeds and none of the dried up stems I usually produce. There is an abundance of colorful blooms. The weather this summer was perfect for neglected dahlias.

This is the bright side of the truism that God never promised us the world would be fair. In a fair world I wouldn't have any flowers to pick this year. We are quick to complain when we get less than we think we deserve. We may not even notice that we sometimes get more.

Whining that the world isn't fair gets us nowhere. Of course it isn't fair. The same rain falls on the just and the unjust and tornadoes don't cleverly focus on the houses of drug dealers. Evil people deceive trusting souls, and clever liars open bank accounts with the wages of sin.

That's good. If a virtuous deed made us an instant lottery winner and even a small sin was quickly followed by a head cold we would all be coerced into decency. Living on the slippery slopes of an unjust world demands more of us.

This unfair world demands that we live by who we are and not by what we think pays off. It asks us to tell the truth not because we will be rewarded for it but simply because it is the truth. It insists that we give without the hope of praise and live a pure life without caring that no one notices.

That makes our choices a little tougher, but at least it's clear what we are choosing.

# Like Deer Caught in the Headlights

The headlights of my car startled a deer one night. Rigid, trembling, it stared at me in frozen silence. I can still remember that deer.

One reason I remember the deer is that I keep seeing its face. Not on deer, on men. I always spent the last moments before a wedding ceremony with the nervous groom. Some of them suddenly realized that an enormous change was taking place in their lives. They were nervous, uncertain and frightened, like a deer caught in the headlights.

From the day we are born great changes alter our lives. Marriages begin and end. Every child becomes an adolescent and then an adult. College leads to commencement, every job ends sometime. Even the family puppy becomes an old dog.

Some changes we seek out. Some we accept if we have the chance. Some we cannot escape. But however change comes it demands an answer. We can choose the answer, but we can't escape the question.

How we answer changes depends on what we believe about who we are and why we are here. If we believe that we are the children of God and are sent here for a purpose no change is a disaster. It is simply a new assignment.

If we believe that the God who sends changes into our lives loves us no change is a threat. It always leads to a happy ending.

I believe in happy endings. I don't believe it by blind faith but by experience. I have seen so many happy endings. When it seems that everything is over it isn't. When it seems that there is no hope there is. When there is nothing we can do we can do one thing. We can wait to see what God brings next.

"Wait on the Lord," the psalmist wrote. These words are not mere poetry. Waiting is one of the hardest things we do. Sometimes we must wait for a very long time. But it is better to wait hopefully than to surrender to despair. There is always a happy ending, in this world or the next.

# Rescuing a Fish

I like to read travel magazines. I'm not so much an armchair traveler as an armchair reminiscer. I like to read about places that I have been. That brings back happy memories.

Not long ago I read an article about Hilo, Hawaii. Hilo hasn't been washed by the killer tides of tourism. The tee shirt shops and crowded resorts are on the other side of the island. Hilo's shores are blessed with lava rocks instead of sandy beaches and that attracts neither tourists nor investments.

Hilo doesn't seem to have changed across the years. One hotel is still the priciest, and the same few restaurants seem to be offering the same food.

My most vivid memory was awakened by a paragraph about restaurants. It said you'd have to drive out of town to reach one eating place. It featured fish freshly caught from private pools outside.

I remember that restaurant or one a lot like it. We went there with two young daughters. As we walked to the entrance we saw a man lying on the sidewalk next to a pool. Suddenly he plunged his arm in the water and threw a wriggling fish on the walk. The chef was going to his watery pantry to start another meal.

For a moment our daughters stopped, startled by this sudden movement. They stared at the flopping fish. Then one of them darted forward, seized the fish by its tail, and threw it back in the pond.

The man jumped to his feet and spoke with conviction in a foreign language. Although we didn't understand his words we got the general drift of his feelings. He was not pleased.

My daughter felt sorry for the fish. The cook thought a demented child was interfering with his job. This was a clash between uncontrolled compassion and the realities of life.

The Bible tells us to love our neighbors. It leaves to us the difficult task of deciding which neighbors to love and which acts are loving. It is good to be compassionate, but it is better to exercise compassion with wisdom.

# The Same Old Adam, in New Clothes

A little girl stood in the corner of the playground, tears making dusty trails down her cheeks. She hadn't fallen in the gravel or been struck by a swing. Her hurt was inside, from words that other children had said to her.

People are sometimes atrociously cruel to one another. The holocaust that slaughtered Jews or the horror that was the Gulag archipelago are unbelievable, but we can't escape belief. They happened.

Bestial behavior wasn't invented in this century. History is rotten with it. But if we didn't originate barbarism we haven't evolved beyond it either. We wear suits instead of skins, but underneath is the same old Adam, doing the same despicable things.

We call such acts "unnatural." We are wrong. They are quite natural in the strictest sense. They are the way nature is. The big fish eat the little fish. The strongest buck rules the herd and fathers the next generation. Cuddly little rodent pets have the dismaying habit of eating their young.

But if we are capable of being animals, that is only part of who we are. We are much more than beasts. We can sacrifice for others; we can give without wanting anything in return. We can control our desires and turn back from unworthy acts. We can forgive and be forgiven.

That is the curse and glory of being human. We are animals, but animals that bear the image of God. The knowledge of good and evil is always with us. We do wrong, but we know that it is wrong. If we can be very bad, we can also be very good.

Animal standards lead to fleeting animal rewards: a full stomach, lusts briefly sated, the exultation of seeing your victim on the ground and your foot upon his neck. That's not much to get out of life.

An old catechism states that the chief end of man is "to glorify God and enjoy Him forever." The second follows from the first. It is only by glorifying God that we can enjoy being more than animals, being the children of our forgiving Maker.

# Elections and Original Sin

Now that the elections are over we can draw a deep breath and sort out our values. We have struck a balance between ideals and morals, we chose between inflated claims and half truths, we made our decisions. These are not easy choices, and many are uneasy with what they chose.

We never have a clear choice between pure good and unmitigated evil. Life is not so simple. No candidate will fulfill our dreams. None will destroy the nation either. No candidate is as good as they claim or as bad as their opponents say they are.

If your candidate wins you are at greater risk than if you vote for the loser. No one will ever know what would have happened if the losers were elected. Winners preserve the opportunity to disappoint us.

Campaigning is a form of mass marketing. It's the number of decisions that count, not the quality of the decisions. The rules for mass marketing are the same in politics as in retailing. They are simple: aim low and use lots of hype. Leave quality and honest words to the niche marketers. Don't worry that you will insult some people's intelligence. Those people are a niche market too.

An election is not a perfect way to choose a country's leaders. It is only the best way. When all the shouting has died down democracy gives us a government that is like us. It reflects our greed and our compassion, our divisions and our unity, our hopes and our fears. It is as selfish as we are and as kind as we are, as wise as our wisdom and as foolish as our foolishness. It is no better than we are, and no worse.

Democracy takes original sin seriously. It is a sensible response to the fact that we are not angels and we do not live in heaven. No one is godlike enough to be our dictator, and no party virtuous enough to rule us.

Heaven doesn't need political campaigns, but we do. We always reserve the right to throw the rascals out -- and put a different set of rascals in.

# Frauds, Fanatics and Fools

Sixty years ago the tent revival was the most exciting thing that happened in small towns. The measure of a successful revival was the noise it made. When I was a boy you could hear a good revival a half mile away.

Some evangelists not overburdened with scruples used shills to boost the sound level. Shills were confederates of the evangelist who were planted in the crowd. Their job was to "get the crowd going". At a signal they produced a holy shout or an impassioned moan. Soon they were joined by the more excitable people around them. Eventually even normal folks gave a whoop or two just to prove they weren't spiritually cold.

It was a minor deception, but religion in every age has attracted frauds, fanatics and fools. Things are done in the name of God that few people would want attached to their own name. Ask the Jews. Always a minority, they have often suffered vicious cruelty sanctified with prayer.

Of course Judaism has had its own frauds, fanatics, and fools. So has Islam, Buddhism, and even the ancient Incas. Shame is an interfaith experience.

Does that mean that religion itself is bad? No more than a savings and loan fraud means that money is bad. It means that religion is powerful, for good or ill, more powerful even than money. When someone invokes God, however understood or misunderstood, an overwhelming force is unleashed. It is power that can be turned to good use or bad.

It is turned to good far more often than it is abused. The power of faith gentles proud spirits, gives the weak strength to survive terrors. It moves hearts to sympathy and compassion. It binds together with love people who are separated by selfishness. This godly power built hospitals and schools before governments thought to do it.

Many people catch a glimpse of the power and glory of God. One wants to seize the glory, another wants to worship it. In the end it comes down to a clear and simple choice.

Do you want to use the power of God, or do you want to be used by it?

# Measured by What We Don't Do

While prowling through the jungle of my computer's software I discovered that there are 281 sounds stored at a dozen different sites on my hard drive. They range from a trumpet fanfare to a car starting with squealing tires. They can be attached to things the computer does, like starting or closing a program.

This looked like a wonderful opportunity. For years my computers have stared at me from a dumb screen, their only sounds whirring fans and an occasional unexplained buzz. Now I could have a computer with personality, entertaining me while it went about its many tasks.

The entertainment didn't last long. I could tolerate the screeching tires for only about an hour. The lion's roar made me jump and look over my shoulder. Insect sounds aroused itching sensations and an urge to call an exterminator. Soon I was shutting sounds off instead of turning them on.

A computer can do a lot of things. Some of them are things you don't want it to do.

Jacques Ellul, a prescient French sociologist and theologian, wrote that it is an axiom of technology that if something can be done it will be. The corollary should be that you don't have to be the one who does it.

There are lots of things that we can do but shouldn't, starting with nuclear weapons and cars that can go over a hundred miles an hour and descending to noisy computers.

Once I bargained inexpertly with a merchant in a Middle Eastern country. He was a better bargainer than I was. We agreed on a price acceptable to both of us, although more acceptable to him than to me I suspect. I thought I counted out the money to pay, but I was unfamiliar with the currency. He shook his head sadly, then counted out the right amount and pushed the rest back to me. Hard bargaining was something he could do and did. Cheating at money was something he could do and wouldn't.

The world measures us by what we can do. God measures us by what we can do and won't.

# The Seminary Bar and Grill

When I was a seminary student in Chicago there was a bar across the street that made a lasting impression on me. They started observing Christmas before Thanksgiving. They put a wreath on the door, strung some lights across the window, and hung speakers outside. The volume on the speakers was turned up to full scream.

This would have been all right, but the only Christmas music they had was a tape of "Rudolph the Red-nosed Reindeer." They blasted this one song endlessly for weeks. If you could hear it as well inside the bar as out it must have led to a lot of heavy drinking. The theology students across the street had to listen while cold sober.

To this day when I hear that song on my car radio I give a convulsive flinch and jab frantically at the control buttons. It is a forgettable tune that I can't forget.

There was something deeply symbolic about that endlessly repeating song outside the seminary gates. It was a foretaste of the problems the students would face later. Christmas would always be a challenge. It wouldn't be easy to remind people of peace on earth and mercy mild while being drowned out by the silly distractions of the holiday season.

The trouble is that Christmas is a great marketing opportunity. We have been told that no one can serve both God and Mammon. The birth of God is the golden opportunity of Mammon. Jesus was a wonderful person, maybe even God the modern mind admits, but at the bottom line Christmas is a business opportunity.

Except that the bottom line is never a number behind a dollar sign. That's a subtotal, important in its own way, unimportant in the scheme of a life. If that's all there is there isn't very much.

The retail sales figures are insignificant to those who are homeless. They are just as useless to all who have houses and cannot find strength for the troubles they face or forgiveness for the past they want to leave behind.

Sometimes you have to ignore the noise to hear the Word.

# Religion that Slips Down Easy

After one of those big, belt-stretching holiday meals my mother always finished with a dessert that was light and airy. "It slips down easy," she would say to her guests, slumped in their chairs in sated torpor.

And it always did. More air than substance, those holiday desserts were as light as a baby's kiss. They demanded nothing from those who had already given their gluttonous all. Eating them was as easy as breathing.

Those desserts wouldn't do for hungry people, of course. They were an airy signature to a meal, not the main course. If they were our only food we would soon be weak and undernourished.

Christmas is prime time for religion that slips down easy. Everyone wants to croon over a baby, and in the traditional pageantry even the sheep look freshly laundered. The stable smells only of new mown hay. There is no need to look for deeper meanings. The simple story is pleasant enough and it makes no demands on us.

That's okay. We've been thinking of deeper meanings all year, stuffed ourselves with heavy fare. Ending the year with something that slips down easy isn't self-indulgence. But if it is the only taste of faith we have all year it won't be enough to nourish our souls.

In this day when faith is marketed like toothpaste the virtues of light and airy religion have long since been discovered. Mass merchandisers of religion know that the biggest market is for the thinnest fare. The less they say the larger their audience is. In the end they will say nearly nothing to almost everyone. They offer meringue for the soul.

Except of course that there are always people who are hungry. They are hurt and don't know where to turn for help. They are disappointed in themselves and don't know how to make a fresh start. They have been knocked down by the sheer brutality of events and long for the strength to stand again.

They are a small group, and don't appear on anyone's marketing plan. But at some time we are all part of that small group.

# It Doesn't Help to Know the Names of Angels

Christmas brings out the best in people, and not just in Christians. The customs of the season gentle everyone. People really enjoy giving, not only to their families, but to the needs of strangers as well. At Christmas we are more likely to discover that enjoyment and be better for the discovery.

Well, not quite everyone. It's best to lock the choir room door on Christmas Eve. We discovered that one holiday when someone rifled the purses of choir members during the midnight service. They were testing the theory that for them at least it might be more blessed to receive and let others give.

But for Christians Christmas is more than a kindly feeling and seasonal generosity. The miracle that began their faith is a miracle we all know: the birth of a baby. The unique event was the most ordinary of events, one we understand and share.

Faith takes place in ordinary events, not in eternal mysteries. It happens in being born and dying, in falling in love and going to work every day. It occurs in classrooms and offices and on buses and in stores. It doesn't help to know the names of angels if you don't know the names of your neighbors.

Faith is not about the next world. It is about how that world is linked to this one. Faith does not just announce that God loves us. It draws the inescapable conclusion: if God loves us, we should love one another. That is something we must do in every day's life, not in our heavenly dreams.

The Christmas story is the oldest story ever told: a man and a woman and a baby spanked squalling into life. The Holy Family is first of all a family like our families.

We sometimes say that Christmas is for children, but that isn't true. In a special way Christmas is for families. It began with a family, and it is with our families that we first experienced it. The highways and airways are crowded with students going home and grandparents going to see their grandchildren.

Families are so ordinary. So is faith.

# A Quarter's Worth of Self Deception

We always hang a calendar on the kitchen wall, and it's time for a new one. I like a calendar with an interesting picture each month, one I will enjoy seeing. That's one reason I have the calendar. The other reason is so I can mark the day when the dog gets his heart worm pill.

All my other reminders are in a desk calendar. The stickers that come with the heart worm pills are too big for the desk calendar. They're too pretty to throw away so I put them on the kitchen calendar.

I should throw them away and write the dates in the desk calendar. I have drawers and closets full of things that are too good to throw away. There are spare bulbs for a flashlight I can no longer find. I have a jar of nuts and bolts that fit no known appliance. I have keys to forgotten locks. Every morning there is a rubber band around my newspaper. I have lots of rubber bands.

These things aren't being recycled. They are being warehoused. If I use them at all it is like I use the dog's stickers. They make my life more complicated instead of easier.

Why do I keep these things? For the same reason that I throw in a quarter every time I pass a Salvation Army kettle. I do it to deceive myself.

For twenty five cents I can believe I am generous and caring. With a drawer full of rubber bands I can believe I am thrifty. Neither act would be convincing to anyone else. They don't have to. I only need to fool myself.

There is a lot of faux virtue of that kind. With an occasional nod to God on Sunday morning I can believe I have faith. With a gift that's too expensive I can believe I love someone. Politicians have the ultimate opportunity for self deception. They can convince themselves that they are moral, idealistic, and love all humankind – and make other people pay for it.

It's not hard to fool ourselves. But we're not likely to fool God. God doesn't count rubber bands.

# Freedom and Responsibility

My dog drinks a lot of water, a bowl full every day. I didn't know this. Taking care of the dog wasn't part of my job description. It took me a while to get his water supply under control. One day the poor creature even carried his empty bowl over to the sink, but he wasn't able to work the tap.

This animal is a responsibility. All he wants is some water, a bowl of food, and a walk at the right time. That's not much responsibility but it's better than none.

Responsibility is the joy of being human, not its burden. God made us only a little lower than the angels, and like angels our life is good when it is useful. We aren't insects who feed and reproduce and die, with no purpose beyond survival. We need to be needed.

Responsibility is more than duty. We owe a duty to someone. We assume responsibility for someone. Duty is imposed on us. Responsibility is joyously chosen. When God made us free to choose how we will live, we were given the glorious capacity to be responsible.

The birth of a child is a terrifying responsibility. The helpless infant needs everything, and the parents are responsible for giving it. When the children are grown the responsibility will be over. The parents may heave a sigh of relief, but the happiest memories they have will be of the years when they were responsible for their family.

We take vows in marriage. When we say those vows we say we are responsible for one another. If the vows are kept they lead to new happiness in each new year. If they are neglected the chance for joy has been thrown away.

The best kind of job is one you can be proud of doing well. A skilled craftsman enjoys seeing his finished work. The person cursed with a mindless job faces daily drudgery and no reward except a pay check.

It is sad to have no responsibility. When we can do whatever we want we soon find that there is very little we want to do. We are not free. We are just unnecessary.

# The Gold at the End of the Rainbow

The Mayo Clinic is in Rochester, Minnesota. Rochester is a small Midwestern town with international visitors. The clocks in the hotel show the time in New York, London, and Dubai. On the streets, Middle Eastern women invisible behind black veils pass Middle Western women with quite visible navels. The local cable television extends beyond the usual English and Spanish channels. Although visitors from the Middle East have diminished greatly in the past year, there are several channels that broadcast in Arabic.

Most of the Arabic channels seem to be either newscasts or speeches by local government officials. One Western show currently appearing is an unexpected choice. It is an Arabic version of a program called "Who Wants to be a Millionaire."

The set and the eerie sound track and the formula are the same. There are the same lifelines: fifty-fifty, ask the audience, phone a friend. The contestants sweat with the same anxiety. The host is a credible equivalent to Regis.

Of all the game shows, situation comedies, and crime programs on American television this is one that has international appeal. The popularity of this show knows no boundaries. Its attraction is simple, unvarnished greed.

To the question, "Who wants to be a millionaire?" the answer is "Me!" The dream of suddenly having wealth is an equal opportunity fantasy. It is older than television, older than history. Every culture has a legend of a leprechaun or a troll or demi-god that guards a pot of gold and will surrender it to someone who can answer a riddle. Television only gives the old tale a modern setting.

Only a romantic who has never been poor doubts that poverty is bad. The hungry people of the world don't enjoy it. But is having a million dollars the secret of happiness? Some lottery winners become desperately unhappy. Some enjoy their good fortune.

If you're happy without being a millionaire, you'd probably be happy if you were. If you are unhappy with a middle class life, winning the million will probably make you no happier. Once the basic needs of life are yours, anything more is irrelevant to your happiness.

Do we all want to be millionaires? Why?

# Anybody Can Quack Like a Duck

Air travel is more complicated than it used to be. When we brought my wife's 90 year old mother from Florida to Illinois we discovered just how complex it could become. Our little group attracted special attention, both good and bad.

The good part was that we didn't have to wait for an hour in the long line before security in the Orlando airport. We were waved to a special section for passengers in wheel chairs and breezed through it quickly. The gate agent agreed to an early boarding, and three of the four in our party entered the plane before the other passengers.

There's no question though that we attracted suspicion. When we went through security my mother-in-law's wheel chair was pulled aside, and she was courteously but thoroughly searched. Her purse and bag were emptied and examined. When the other three boarded the plane I was stopped and waved to one side. I took off my shoes as I was directed. I submitted to a scan of my body. I waited while my bag was emptied and each item carefully examined. I was the last person to get on the plane.

An elderly lady of impeccable manners in a wheel chair seems an unlikely terrorist. So does a Swedish-American of senior years. The random search seemed to ignore possible dangers in pursuing unlikely ones. It seemed we were the victims of mindless bureaucrats following orders.

Maybe we weren't. We know that terrorists are not stupid. They plan carefully to accomplish their murderous intent. Maybe our selection was not random at all. Maybe it was the result of profiling. We may have been chosen because we fit a suspicious pattern.

If I were trying to smuggle weapons aboard a plane I wouldn't send a swarthy young man wearing a towel around his head. I would use a well-dressed older lady in a wheel chair, perhaps without her knowledge. Or I might form a family group, disguising myself with make-up and hair dye as an elderly Swede. Either would work.

We were innocent of course. Not everything that quacks is a duck. Maybe we were victims of profiling. It beats being the victims of killers.

# Perfection Would Be a Bore

I've owned a lot of cars, but there are a few I remember with special affection. The first car I owned needed to be loved. It was a used car that had been used a lot. It had loveable eccentricities, like a gasoline gauge that always showed empty and a tendency to stall at inconvenient times. While I owned it the color was changed from green to black, after an error in judgment on an icy road. The engine, which had suffered greatly, finally collapsed. It was replaced by a rebuilt motor from a different car.

Most of my cars had names. That first car was named by my fraternity brothers, who called it "The Padre-mobile", in honor of the profession for which I aimed. One of them cherished a vehicle bought from a funeral director. It had been repainted a lurid purple, and was known as "The Hearse of a Different Color."

Almost as memorable was "The White Queen." The Queen was a huge station wagon. She was previously owned by a friend who didn't want to surrender her to the mercy of strangers. The Queen was addicted to drink and seldom passed a gas station without stopping for a quick one. Her cavernous interior was great for carrying Christmas trees, large dogs, and bags of fertilizer. She was used for all those things, and on a calm day you could smell them.

Eventually I grew up and started driving ordinary cars which had no personality at all. When you turned the key the engine started and when you turned the key off the engine stopped. This took a lot of the uncertainty out of driving. That's when I stopped giving my cars names.

My car was no longer a quirky friend, whose odd habits were familiar. It was just a car, a means of transportation. My car was reliable. Reliability is good, but it's not the stuff that dreams are made of.

We are not perfect, and it's too much to hope that we will be. We are forgiven, and that's better. We wouldn't need to be forgiven if we were perfect. We would be useful but boring, and nobody would love us.

# Las Vegas for the Elderly

When you are nursing a broken leg you can read all day without feeling guilty. That's great – for about two days. When you are reading cereal boxes for entertainment you know you've reached the end of your resources.

That's when I volunteered to help at a retirement home. I offered to do anything that can be done sitting down, preferably with one leg raised. I discovered that I was qualified to call the numbers for a Bingo game. Bingo in a retirement center isn't exactly Las Vegas, so I felt sure I could do it. It would demonstrate my compassion for the lame, the halt, and the merely old. How hard could it be to play Bingo with a group of elderly people?

It can be harder than you think. I found myself in a room with four other volunteers and about twenty gamblers, all of whom apparently came every week and were experienced at Bingo.

One man indicated that he was a graduate of the law school in my home town, and quizzed me about several professors he knew. I didn't know any of them. I had the distinct impression that he suspected me of being an impostor.

His suspicions were deepened when he discovered that I knew very little about Bingo. My memories of the game from childhood were of a simple game that was only slightly more complicated than Candyland.

There are, it appears, a great many variations on the traditional game. Everyone there but me knew about Big Picture Frame and Little Picture Frame, Layer Cake and North-South. I didn't even know what the goal of each game was, let alone being able to decide who won.

Verifying winners was hard. My lawyer friend read his numbers very fast and in random order. I'm still not sure if he really won.

The group was equally divided between those who wanted me to call the numbers faster and those who wanted me to repeat the last three numbers because they were falling behind.

I came to show that I was compassionate. I discovered that I needed the compassion of others. I was just glad that they didn't make me play for money.

# We Are What We Watch

The television we watch tells a lot about us. For instance, this year there are several shows about law enforcement. This is an old theme, going back to the sheriffs and marshals of western movies. Today's crime fighter is not a tall man on a horse, though. Nobody stands loose-jointed at the OK Corral waiting for the moment of truth. The hero is more likely to be looking into a microscope than across a gun sight. The violence is in the crime, not in the arrest.

That doesn't mean the shows are bloodless. The camera lingers over the mutilated bodies of victims. We see things once viewed only by pathologists. We don't hear autopsy reports. We watch the autopsy. The viewer doesn't need to have much imagination. Nothing is left to be imagined.

We've come a long way from the early days of television. In those days there were gun fights in which dozens of shots were fired but the heroes were never killed. At worst they were shot in the arm and appeared later with a sling. If wounds were inflicted we weren't required to look at them. The show generally ended with someone riding off into the sunset.

Today's shows aim at being more realistic, but in fact neither kind of show is much like real life. Very few people have ever seen a gunfight or a murder. Those who live in drug-ridden places where such things happen probably don't find it entertaining. Only those who are far away from the violence want to see it in their living room.

Even terrorism hasn't brought horrors into every life. Despite the mass killings of people who hate, they are not our greatest threat. We are in more danger from a neighbor with a driver's license and a drinking habit than from a wild-eyed fanatic.

Genuine realism doesn't make good drama. There is more quiet desperation than valiant sacrifice in real life. The streets are generally calm. Villains don't ride horses into town firing their pistols. They just falsify the books.

In real life sin is real, but it isn't exciting. Despite what you see on television, most of our sins are simply boring.

# A Sudden Change in Life

What do you do when the world falls apart? How can we go on when the veneer of civilization by which we live – the "thou shalts" and "thou shall nots" – crack open and the unthinkable must be thought?

It happens. A crazed youth on a college campus or a zealot strapped with explosives in Baghdad destroy the fragile certainties that make civilized life possible. The calculated cruelties of the concentration camp violate our confidence in humanity. Heartless genocide and unbridled terrorism break down the barriers that keep out chaos.

These events always raise questions we cannot answer. But there are a few questions we can answer, little patches of solid ground on which we can keep our footing.

The first is that there is no perfect defense against unmitigated evil. No law will restrain the lawless. No appeals to decency will deter those already outside decency's bounds. We can never be sure that we are safe, at any time, in any place.

There is good news however. In every shocking tragedy there are heroes as well as destroyers, and the heroes outnumber the destroyers. The elderly professor throws his body against the door so the students can escape. The fire fighter goes into the falling building without thinking of her personal cost. When events are determined by the worst in humanity, the best that was hidden comes out. In the end love rules: that love than which there is none greater. People do willingly lay down their lives for another.

Unimaginable tragedy forces us to decide who we are and what we want to be. It either drives us together or forces us apart. We either strike out fearfully at everyone around or reach comforting arms to all the others.

In terrible times we do not look for strength to the engineers or theologians. It is the poets and musicians who know the language of the unspeakable. Hymns say things that sermons cannot. The deep truths that save us are not found in a user's manual.

"… and when the fight is fierce, the warfare long
Steals on the ear the distant triumph song
And hearts are brave again, and arms are strong."

# But What if I am Wrong?

We are warned not to operate heavy machinery while we are under the influence of a cold medicine. I don't have any problem with this. I've seen what a bull dozer or backhoe can do. I don't want any part of it. Anything heavier than a bicycle is too much responsibility for me.

Most people know better than to operate a crane when they are full of antihistamines. Sometimes they take even bigger risks with religion. Religious faith is a powerful force. Because it is powerful, faith is dangerous. Faith can bless. It can also destroy.

For many people, faith keeps their life in balance. It stabilizes them. It helps them survive hard times without despair and enjoy good times without becoming proud. Because of faith they trust the will of God, even though they don't know where that trust will lead them. That's safe enough.

For others faith is the power that makes them live unselfishly. They rush into an endangered building to save the life of another. They give up comforts to serve in the slums of Calcutta or New York. These are not rational choices. They are made with the heart, not the mind.

Faith is always related to the will of God: trusting it or serving it. That's where the danger lies. It is not easy to know what the will of God is. Those who are certain they know are the most dangerous of all. They unleash the tremendous power of faith heedlessly.

That's where suicide bombers come from. It is also the reason why nice people often do nasty things when they fight in their church or synagogue. The claim that it pleases God can whitewash the most ungodly behavior. There is a fine line between wanting to live for God and wanting to hurt God's enemies. Persecuting heretics and infidels has always been popular. How can it be wrong to do God's will?

The more deeply committed we are to our religion, the more important it is that we ask a simple question: What if I am wrong? That could moderate our anger in this life, and save us from an unpleasant surprise in the next.

# Let's Move Christmas to June

It's too bad that Christmas comes during the holiday season. There is so much going on that it is hard to enjoy any of it. Maybe we should have Christmas at a quieter time, like the end of June. Nothing much happens at the end of June.

December is a busy month. It is near the end of the year, and we have the IRS breathing down our neck. There are things we do every year and can't stop doing now. We have presents to wrap, parties to go to (and maybe host), cards to send and decorations to deploy. If we move Christmas to June there will have to be some rules. There will be no Christmas cards, no decorations, no parties, and nobody will send or receive gifts. We could do all those things in December. In June there would just be Christmas and we would have time to enjoy it.

This isn't the usual plea to make Christmas more religious by shucking off all the worldly distractions. A lot of the worldly distractions are good, but we don't have time to enjoy them either. There's nothing particularly religious about bringing our scattered families together. We often do that at Christmas, but we're too busy to really enjoy it. Everybody arrives exhausted from jumping through the seasonal hoops. If we moved Christmas, I'd still like to have families get together.

I like food, and there's a lot of good food at Christmas time. It would be nice though it if we could enjoy it without the cooks being breathless, their eyes glazed with fatigue. If we have Christmas in June, I'd still like to have Christmas dinner. There's nothing religious about it, but it doesn't do any harm either.

Families and food are the two things I would move to June along with Christmas. All of the other things that keep us so busy could stay in December. That would be enough to keep us dazed and harried and keep the economy humming. We could even declare a special, non-Christmas December holiday. It would be the kind of holiday the Civil Liberties Union could love. It would have no religious meaning whatever.

# The Half-Life of a Sermon

Last week I watched an artist who produced work that has to be seen quickly. It doesn't last long. It is more permanent than blowing soap bubbles, but not by much.

I saw him at the Chicago Botanical Society. This is an expansive tract of gardens that isn't in Chicago, but in a North Shore suburb called Highland Park. I suppose the Highland Park Botanical Society wouldn't attract much attention.

It's crowded in summer, when the flowers are in bloom. It is crowded now, because for a month before Christmas they have a celebration. Hundreds of trees and shrubs are decked with lights. Topiary trees and shrubs, accented with banks of white flowers, fill the indoor rooms. Red is used sparingly, but with great effect. In one greenhouse a giant ball of blooming poinsettias hangs from the ceiling.

To bring a crowd they add musicians, story tellers, and carriage rides through the park. There is food, both casual eating and fine dining. Volunteers help visitors make a topiary tree of sorts, a sort of Martha Stewart approach to landscape gardening.

One of the attractions is an ice sculptor. He attacks a giant block of ice; first with a chain saw, then with chisel and hammer. We watched his progress through the evening, as he fashioned a life size representation of the Madonna and Child. It was an impressive work, exquisitely detailed.

Sculpting ice is probably good for the artist's soul. He doesn't think he is a Rodin or Michelangelo. Neither bitter nor frustrated, he doesn't blame his lack of recognition on the tastelessness of common people. Like people who preach sermons, he has chosen a medium that has a very short half-life, and he knows it.

The world is full of people who think they possess great genius but do not. Their longing for importance frustrates them and annoys everyone around. The ice sculptor is quite happy doing well something very few people can do at all. He doesn't hope for enduring fame.

There is a reason why each of us is here. It doesn't matter whether we were born to carve in marble or in ice. We just need to do it well.

# The Innocent Dream of Santa Claus

I want to say a good word for Santa Claus. Kris Kringel has no religious value, but he deserves better than a job selling soda pop and miscellaneous toys.

Most children today wouldn't recognize a sugar plum if their mom put one in their lunch. They are familiar with the UPS truck, but they have never seen reindeer making house calls. The notion of a fat man in a red suit dropping down the chimney is ludicrous. Even if the house has a fireplace, the flu is too small for anything bigger than a starling, and it is probably capped with a screen to keep birds out.

On the night before Christmas one creature is stirring after the children are tucked into bed. It is Dad, frantically searching for Slot 42, so the he can insert Tab J and put together the Super Space Station (some assembly required.)

Still, the old poem is a lot more appealing than what really happens. Reindeer power doesn't pollute the air and it requires no imports from unstable Middle Eastern kingdoms. The mysterious stranger with the white beard is fun. The harried cash register jockey in a crowded superstore isn't.

We continue to delight in hearing about the jolly old elf and his eight tiny reindeer because the story is a happy one. It is an innocent dream, telling children that the world is not a place of terrors after all. It is a place where they are loved, where good surprises wait for them.

Children learn early about the dark side of life. They are taught to never get in a car with a stranger, not to take candy from someone they don't know. They are warned that even a trusted adult may abuse them. They need to know these things.

But they also need to know that this is only part of the world around them. The dangers are real, but they are not the only reality. Children need to know that love is as true as evil, and that goodness is as sure as danger.

The poem is truthful, but not literally true. Sometimes a good story tells more truth than naked facts.

# Life that Is Painful, Noisy and Messy

For several years when I was a small boy I had a role in a Christmas play at our church. It wasn't exactly a speaking part. It was more of an eating part. The one thing I remember is that I was to pick up a loaf of freshly baked bread, tear chunks out of it, and eat them. This probably meant something profound, but I've forgotten what it was. It was pretty good bread though, and that's what I remember. For me, Christmas was the taste of freshly baked bread.

I suppose the point of that play was to present "the real meaning of Christmas." Every year there is a lot of talk about that real meaning, which always seems in danger of being lost. Part of the problem is that everybody has a different idea of what the real meaning is. For some it is the spirit of giving. For others it is peace and good will. There are some who feel the real meaning is expressed by simplicity and self denial. The possibilities are endless.

All of these real meanings are abstract. They are desirable qualities, but they are not attached to anything specific and real. They are ideas, not things that happen in the world.

It is strange we should think any of them are the meaning of Christmas. The story of Christmas is anything but abstract. It is about a woman giving birth to a child in a stable. Childbirth is a painful, noisy, messy business. There is nothing more this-worldly than that.

Life is often painful, noisy, and messy. We come into the world that way, and may leave with the same untidiness. In the years between we encounter greed and generosity, healing and destroying, nobility and consummate evil. We not only encounter all these things, we participate in them. Life is complicated, and so are we.

When we describe Christmas in sweet abstractions we are not moving closer to its real meaning. We are moving farther away. We are moving away from the sights and sounds and smells of that stable. Real meanings are not described. They are experienced, and the experiences are deeper than words.

# They Cry Peace When There Is No Peace

The First World War was called "The War to End All Wars". The victorious allies tried to guarantee that hope by imposing a draconian peace on Germany. Strict limits were placed on German arms, the Saar Valley was declared a demilitarized zone, and small new democratic countries like Czechoslovakia replaced the Austrian empire. They didn't foresee the rise to power of Adolph Hitler.

In 1935 Hitler marched his troops into the Saar. At that point Germany was not yet strong enough to be a threat. It was the first test of European resolve, and particularly of the League of Nations. The League failed the test, and there was no response to Hitler.

In 1937 Hitler took control of Austria. Again there was no response. In 1938 Germany claimed ownership of the Sudetenland, border regions of Czechoslovakia with a sizeable ethnic German population.

The British Prime Minister, Neville Chamberlain, hurried to meet with Hitler in his mountain retreat at Berchtesgaden. He met Hitler's demands, claimed that the German need for land had been "appeased", and said that he had achieved "peace in our time." Within months Hitler occupied the rest of Czechoslovakia.

Peace was a popular cause in Britain in the thirties. The Oxford Union debated whether it was right to die "for God and Country", and God and Country lost. During this period America had its own peace movement. Every Midwestern county seat town had a chapter of the isolationist American First Committee. Prominent citizens, including not only politicians but popular heroes like Charles Lindberg, supported the movement. The Fellowship of Reconciliation mobilized religious groups to oppose the use of force under any circumstances.

In 1939 Hitler invaded Poland. World War II officially began. It had actually been under way for four years.

During those four years Germany rearmed and became powerful enough to conquer most of Europe. Defeating Hitler's armies was exceedingly difficult and the outcome was uncertain. Thousands of soldiers died unnecessarily when the delayed war resumed. Thousands of civilians suffered the brutality of Nazi justice unnecessarily. Thousands of Jews died unnecessarily in the death camps.

Of course, Saddaam Hussein may be a much nicer person than Adolf Hitler.

# Helen Jo's Pony

I have owned a lot of dogs and a lot of cars, and I have happy memories of both. With both dogs and cars the one I enjoyed the most was my first one.

My first car was a hard-used sedan that was green when I bought it and black after I rolled it over on a slippery highway. My first dog was an over-active clown of highly mixed parentage. He had characteristics of so many breeds it was impossible to assign him to any one or two.

Neither the dog nor the car was beautiful. I treasured them for only one reason: they were mine. I had never owned a dog or a car before, and I was happy, happy to own one now.

No later car or dog brought that same delight. They were good cars and dogs, but the joy of that first possession couldn't be repeated.

I remember lots of firsts. I remember my first date with a girl. I remember the first time I fell in love, long before that first date. It was the summer before I was in sixth grade. Her name was Helen Jo, and she had a pony cart in which she let me drive her around town. My heart was moved. I'm not sure whether I loved Helen Jo or the pony, but I knew lots of girls and only one pony.

I remember the first sermon I preached, at a little English church called Mile End Chapel. After the service one of the elders told me I hadn't talked long enough. That was a complaint I never heard again.

I remember the birth of my first child and my first grandchild. The other children were as wonderful, but we crossed into new country with the first ones.

All of these first things are alike in one way. Although we may have looked forward to them, when they happened they were richer and more wonderful than we imagined.

Some people think they know exactly what heaven will be like. I hope I don't. I hope that it will be like all the other first things: a wondrous surprise, a world beyond our earthbound dreams.

# A Car Named Edsel

Many decades ago the Ford motor company brought out a new car. This event, which the press agents rated just below the discovery of America and well above the invention of Scotch tape, needed a name worthy of its importance. The company hired a famous poet to choose the name.

She made a good effort. She looked at drawings of the car and asked about its attributes. She looked up words in a Latin dictionary; she browsed through Roget and Bartlett. Finally she submitted four names to the company.

They paid her, thanked her profusely, and then told her they had already decided on a name. They would name it for one of the founder's descendants. They called it the Edsel.

Having an automobile named for you isn't a ticket to enduring fame. People who know the car usually don't know anything about the person. Louis Chevrolet and Walter Chrysler were famous in their day, but few people who drive their cars know who they were. R.E. Olds won't be forgotten when the last Oldsmobile rolls off the assembly line. He was forgotten a long time ago.

It turned out even worse for Edsel Ford. The Edsel, which was distinguished by a grill that resembled a trout sucking a lemon, had a short and inglorious history. It was bought mainly by people with poor judgment and worse taste. Rather than honoring the man named Edsel, they linked his name to one of the great commercial failures of the century.

In Old Testament times the name of God was so revered that no one would say it. When it was written in scrolls, the speaker would say aloud an entirely different word, one which meant "The Lord."

Cheapening the name of God is forbidden by one of the Ten Commandments. Fortunately no one has named a car for God, but we have done everything else to break the commandment. One religionist has even asked what kind of car God would drive. This reduces God to a car salesman.

We have lost our sense of the holy. We respect no one, are awed by nothing, honor no superior. That's too bad. When nothing is sacred, everything is ugly.

# Prices and Priceless

Restaurants try to tell you good things about their food. Some have menus with color pictures. Some print descriptions: ("hickory broiled, with a delicate lemon-dill sauce.") Many rely on the waiter's ability to describe the special of the evening with salivating enthusiasm. ("I'm Todd. I'll be your waiter tonight.")

Sometimes the dish lives up to its description. Sometimes it doesn't. Your disappointment is in direct proportion to the price you paid for the meal. Nobody complains about a fast food hamburger, but you expect more from Todd.

It is sad to not be able to get what you want. It is sadder to get what you want, and find that you don't like it. That is the tragedy that haunts the Western world.

We have an abundance of things we want, far more than most of the world. Our streets are crowded with automobiles. Our malls and big box stores are crammed with electronics, clothing, appliances, and cosmetics. All these wonders don't stay in the shop long. They stream in from tractor trailers in back of the store, and stream out to cars in front of the store.

We are better housed, better fed, and better entertained than our parents dreamed of being. The rich live like sultans. The poor of this country live better than the middle class in many places. We have everything we need and many things we don't need.

Yet somehow the abundance never satisfies us. We have what we wanted, and now we don't want it. There is a blank place in our life, and nothing we buy will fill it.

Despite the claims of politicians, the problem isn't the economy. Our happiness won't be fulfilled by double digit growth of the GNP, the DJI, or our IRA's. There are people who are happy and fulfilled who don't know what GNP or DJI mean. There are people who know altogether too much about such alphabetical measures who will never have enough.

Why do people who have so much feel vaguely dissatisfied? They don't have everything. They only have a lot of the things that money can buy. The priceless things of life are still out of their reach.

# The Times are A-changing

Everything changes, even something as timeless as a church. Whether the change is good or not depends on two things: what it is that is changed, and what it is changed to become. Those two factors make the difference between a supportive faith and a dangerous cult.

Businesses have to change, too. Those that don't change soon become out of date and disappear. A business consultant writes that for a company it isn't just one kind of change, it is three kinds. People have to change in their head, in their heart, and in their hands. Two out of three won't work.

Our head is what we think with. Our hands are what we work with. Changing head and hands means changing the way we think and the way we act. That's our strong suit. We are very good at thinking and doing. We are analytic thinkers and pragmatic doers. That's the American way.

Changing our hearts is different. That isn't about thinking or acting. It is about caring and being. We aren't so good at that. We can state our thoughts and compare them with other thinking. We can measure the effects of what we do. A change of heart can't be measured or compared to anything else. It goes outside the world of measurements where we are so comfortable.

That's the problem of our age. We are very good with our hands and our heads. We are not doing so well with our hearts.

We have all benefited from research and technology. Those are head and hands things, and because we do them well our lives are richer, more varied, and more comfortable than any generation before us. We have made a bargain with the technicians. We will believe whatever can be measured, tested and proven. We will not believe anything else. We will believe our head and hands. We will doubt our hearts.

But we cannot escape the questions that can't be answered with heads and hands. Questions like, "Why were we born?" "What is love?" "What will happen when we die?" These are questions about things we can't measure. Unless our heart is changed, changing our head and hands won't be enough.

# The First Driver's License

Graduation and marriage are big turning points in life. In a few moments one part of life is left behind, never to be seen again. Nothing is the same as it was before. But there is another event that changes everything, one that comes before either graduation or marriage. It is the day of an adolescent's first driver's license.

Parents, who have worried about their children from birth, now have a new reason to worry. Instead of wondering if their offspring will get places on time, they hope they will get there safely. On the other hand, another driver in the family means a new freedom for at least one adult. After years of being a chauffeur she no longer needs to drive to every soccer match, dentist appointment, and play practice.

It means a different kind of freedom for the new drivers. They probably won't drive very much for a while. There's a line waiting to use the family car, and the teen is at the end of the line. But just having the license is liberating. No longer bound to travel on foot or bicycle, there is a whole new world of freedom. You know that you could drive anywhere, even if you don't get a chance to do it.

The car keys, which were barely noticed before, become a family icon. To have them dropped into a teen-ager's palm is like the touch of the king's sword on the shoulder of a new knight. They are looked at with longing and accepted with joy.

If the new driver is a boy the family insurance premiums soar. Girls are deemed less of a risk. It is a matter of hormonal balance. To a boy driving a car is a symbol of burgeoning manhood. To a girl it is a convenient way to get to the mall. Without testosterone an automobile is only a means of transportation.

Life is a series of abrupt changes. Those driven by others suddenly become drivers. Students in a brief ceremony stop being students. Children become parents. Every change in our lives means not only entering a world we never knew before, but leaving behind one we will never enter again.

# The Difference Between Awesome and Awe

The temples of ancient Egypt and the cathedrals of medieval Europe were alike in one way. They were built on such a grand scale that even today they make visitors catch their breath at their immensity. Walk beneath those towering pillars and soaring arches and you feel humbled. You sense that you are in the presence of something holy beyond your imagining.

Although the gods they worshiped were very different, the response to them was the same. These temples and cathedrals were designed to express awe. Awe is the starting point of all religion. Faith is our response to knowing that there is a reality that is grander, wiser, and more powerful than we can imagine. It is our response to awe.

We don't build such cathedrals or temples any more. Our places of worship are more likely to express practicality than awe. They are this-worldly buildings, designed to be useful to us. Instead of reaching toward the inaccessible stars they look no higher than we can easily touch.

We talk about awe more and experience it less than any generation before us. Anything we like we call awesome: a movie, an athlete, a new car, a new kind of ice cream. We have shrunk the word so that instead of being as immense as God it is as small as we are. It doesn't mean that we feel awe. We don't.

What we feel may be pleasure or satisfaction or admiration. It isn't awe. Awe peers into eternity. We peer into our own feelings. Instead of looking up we look in. We are concerned about what we feel, not what eternity is.

Although we don't talk about it, we still feel awe. We feel it when we stand inside those cathedrals or temples. We feel it when we look at a newborn child, our newborn child. We feel it when we look up at the stars on a summer night. We feel it every time we are confronted with beauty so wonderful it overwhelms us. We feel it when we reach the edge of what we know and see that there is still mystery beyond.

Such moments are as awesome as they are uncommon.

# Japanese Wrestlers at the Movies

Movies make me think of popcorn, and popcorn makes me thirsty. On the way into the theater I stopped at the concession stand. I asked for two small soft drinks and some popcorn.

"Get a number four," the concession clerk said. "It costs less."

A number four turned out to be two magnums of soft drink and popcorn in a tub big enough to use for a dog bath. All I wanted was a snack for a movie. I had enough food for a trek across the Mojave Desert.

One of the odd trends in Western society is the continuing inflation of junk food portions. Soft drinks that were once a standard nine ounces grew to twelve ounces, then sixteen, and now are measured in liters. Two hamburgers were put in a bun, then three and growing. Once there were small, medium and large sizes. Small disappeared, medium became regular and large exploded into an ascending hierarchy of super sizes.

While part of the world starves, obesity is a major health risk in other places. This isn't just an American problem. Television shows us street scenes in Europe. Germans waddle into their beer halls, Brits and Italians and Greeks strain against their belts. With the exception of professional athletes and actors everyone is expanding like a gaseous substance. Diets and exercise programs have become an international obsession. Never have so many sacrificed so greatly with so little effect.

Junk food is blamed because of its excessive calories. Actually it isn't just the quality of snacks that is to blame. It is the quantity. Eating and drinking this much of almost anything would turn us into Japanese wrestlers.

Restaurants offer "all you can eat" specials. Nobody should eat all they can eat. You shouldn't even let your dog eat all he can eat.

The name for all this eating is gluttony, one of the seven mortal sins. It is not just bad manners, it is morally wrong. The book of Proverbs suggests a cure: if you have a big appetite put a knife to your throat. That should solve the problem, but there must be a less drastic way.

All I wanted was a little popcorn.

# Point and Click

Cameras have improved so much that almost anyone can take pretty good pictures. Point-and-shoot cameras produce photos that are in focus. They adjust for the light, and do fairly well many of the things professionals do better. The pictures may not be of the highest quality, but they're good enough to bring back memories of trips and games and relatives and all the other things that warm our hearts when we recall them.

We're not likely to have a professional photographer around for all the scenes we want to preserve. The moment when the graduate reaches out for the diploma will probably be photographed by a family member, not a professional. That scene of the family grinning at the camera with Niagara Falls in the background is captured by one of us or it is lost forever. The one indispensable trait of the photographer is simply to be there, and it is usually an amateur who is there.

The second most important trait of a photographer is to remember to take a picture. That's the part I have a problem with. I always take a camera on trips. I carry one to memorable moments in family life, like weddings and baptisms. When I get home I wonder why I took so few pictures.

The problem is that I get interested in where we are and what is happening, and I forget about the camera. As a result the only views I bring home are of places, people and events I didn't find interesting. I produce small albums of boring pictures.

It doesn't matter how good the camera is if nobody pushes the little round button. All the skill of the camera makers is wasted without that last step: taking the picture. Some of the most important pictures of our families are the ones nobody remembered to take.

Each of those pictures I didn't take was a wasted opportunity. I can't go back and take them now. I can't ever take them.

Prayers are like photographs. If we don't say them now we can't say them later. It may be that our most important prayers are the ones we should have said and didn't.

# Poe and the Bird

I've always thought that Edgar Allen Poe was a little unstable. He wrote a very long poem about a raven. Poe claimed that late one night this strange bird tapped on his study window. When Poe opened the window the bird flew into the room. The raven sat on a plaster bust and mournfully repeated the word, "nevermore." When I had to read this in high school I decided that Poe was smoking something he shouldn't that night.

I'm not so sure now. A demented bird keeps tapping on my study window. He is a cardinal, not a raven, a much prettier bird. But he tapped on my window all morning. I went to lunch, and when I came back the bird was there again, tapping. I have not opened the window. I am afraid the bird will talk to me.

If that bird talks to me I will know I am over medicated. That would not surprise me. Most people are over medicated today. We live in the Age of Pills and Capsules. Television commercials urge us to ask our doctor if more drugs "are right" for us. Sometimes the ads don't even tell us what disease the drug is supposed to treat. They just say we should ask our doctor if it's right for us.

Your doctor will tell you that there is more to good health than pills. There is no pharmaceutical substitute for exercise and a healthy diet. Even the healthiest life style however doesn't lead to immortality. Neither do medicines, but they can ward off some dangers and relieve some symptoms. We live longer and enjoy it more because of the advances in medical care, including the pills and capsules prescribed for us.

That's all they will do, though. There is more to life than good health. Some of the happiest people are those who have overcome the greatest physical obstacles. Many great things are achieved by people who aren't feeling very well at the time.

Living longer is no blessing if the added years are empty of meaning. Man does not live by bread alone. Pills aren't enough either. There is no pill that will make your soul healthy.

# We Are All Amateurs

You can learn a lot from the Internet. For example, I learned from the Wabash Valley E-Mail News one way to stay awake when I'm driving. A former truck driver offered a simple solution: open the driver's side window and hold a hundred dollar bill outside in your left hand.

Of course he's a professional driver. I have to give the standard warning: don't try this at home. It's not for amateurs. You may lose more than your hundred dollars.

The mark of the true professional is that they make difficult tasks look easy. Whether they're playing golf, performing eye surgery, or driving in a stock car race they seem to be doing it effortlessly, naturally, easily. You may even think, "I can do that!" You can't.

The difference between the professional and the amateur is not that the professional has superior gifts. All ability is a gift, but the professional is one who has developed the gift. The professional has studied and practiced until learned skills become habits. The professional has shaped and honed his natural gift until it is as good as it can be made. The professional has paid the price for exceptional performance.

We are all amateurs at most of the things we have to do, even some that are very important. Children are raised by amateur parents. By the time they finish the job they know a lot more than before they started, but it is too late.

Being a grandparent is an altogether different role. If grandparents think they know a lot about parenting they would be wise to keep their knowledge to themselves. They're on the sidelines now, and the one thing that serious participants don't need is shouted advice from the sidelines.

We are all amateurs at faith, even those whose profession is religion. There is no direct connection between studying religion and experiencing it. As in anything else we have to pay the price for exceptional performance. The price is practicing what we know until it becomes natural and looks easy.

I have my own technique for fighting off sleep while driving. If you have to fight to stay awake, don't do it. Stop driving.

# Stomach Pumps at the Dinner Table

The easy way to get mushrooms is to buy them at the grocery store, but some people like to hunt them in the wild. Morels are especially prized. Mushroom hunters usually know some secret place where this elusive fungus can be found. Presumably they also know which mushrooms are morels and which only look like morels. The difference is important.

There is no antidote for mushroom poisoning. This leads to a lot of graveyard humor among mushroom fanciers, such as "You can eat any fungus you find in the woods, but some kinds you can only eat once."

One web site devoted to morels warns that if you feel dizzy, nauseous, or cramping after eating wild mushrooms you should go at once to the nearest emergency room and "ask for a stomach pump in your size."

This takes something away from gracious dining. It is hard to enjoy the delicate flavor of mushrooms when you're thinking about stomach pumps. Nothing tastes very good when you're afraid it might be lethal.

There are enough uncertainties in life without bringing one to the dinner table. We are at risk from ancient plagues that have desolated continents and from viruses that were unknown the day before yesterday. On any day we may encounter a terrorist in the skies or a drunken assassin on the highway.

We don't know what will happen in the next hour, let alone the next year. We may win the lottery, but there is just as good a chance that we will learn that we have cancer. Some things happen to us because of what we do. Some happen because of what other people do. Some things just happen.

Life is uncertain, but not random. We are not the victims of things that happen for no particular reason. We are the children of a loving God, born for a purpose, bound for a destination. Faith believes that life makes sense, even when we can't see the sense of it. Murderous mushrooms, drunken drivers, and even lottery tickets all fit together in a plan. We can see some of the plan in this world, and in the next world we will see it all.

# The Danger of Freedom

My parents, who were born in Sweden, were naturalized American citizens. My father liked to tell about the day his citizenship was granted. The aspirants appeared before a judge, who gave them a brief and unscientific oral examination. One man failed because he didn't know that Harrisburg is the capital of Pennsylvania. This wouldn't have been so bad if the court weren't in Pittsburgh.

They chose to be Americans. It was their second big decision. The first was when they decided to come here to live. They didn't think they would ever see their home again. They did in fact return to visit relatives a few years later. By then they were foreigners in their native land. When they came back to America they were coming home.

I didn't do anything to become an American. I didn't choose it and I didn't work to make it possible. I became an American citizen while bawling and mewling in the hospital where I was born. It was a gift.

I was lucky, but my parents were luckier. Their gift was not American citizenship. It was being given a choice. They were free to choose where they would live and what loyalty they would have.

I made none of these decisions. I had no joyful memory of a Pennsylvania court room, no special delight in the Fourth of July. I simply accepted what I was. They chose who they would be.

The freedom to choose is the best gift life can offer. It is a dangerous gift, as all great gifts are, because we may choose badly. We may choose selfishness over service, greed over charity, shallow pleasure over deep commitment. But if we couldn't make that choice there would be no service or charity or commitment. There would only be acceptance.

When we see great evil we may wonder why, if there is a God, God permits it. God doesn't permit it. God gives the freedom to choose, and some choose one way and some the other. Osama Bin Laden is the price we pay to have Mother Theresa. Both were driven by religion. They were free to choose how to express their faith.

# Michael Jordan's Voice

The Internet Service Provider I use offers a number of utterly useless features. For example, I can change the voice that tells me I've "got" mail. A number of celebrities are offered. Currently I'm using Michael Jordan. Not because he's a great basketball player, but because he has a pleasant voice that combines friendliness with dignity. He makes me feel that it might actually be worth looking at all that junk e-mail. The feeling doesn't last very long.

Friendliness and dignity don't always go together. Actors, politicians, and television anchors are practiced at friendliness. Some are so affectionate you feel they'd like to curl up in your lap and purr. Dignity is not uncommon among university professionals, morticians, and the clergy. None of these are invariably cuddly.

Friendliness or dignity taken separately can be a little cloying. Together they become quite pleasant. They aren't separate aspects of the same person, who is now friendly and now dignified. They are both in constant play, each holding the other in tension, saving friendliness from being silly and dignity from being aloof. Friendliness needs dignity, and dignity cries out for friendliness.

Many things that seem to be opposites aren't. We shouldn't try to choose between peace and justice. Peace without justice submits to tyranny. Justice untempered by peace justifies cruelty. We need to be tugged by our desire for peace and our need for justice, with our view of each shaped by the other. We need as much peace as we can have with justice, and as much justice as we can have with peace. We probably won't have either perfectly. We could only have perfect peace by forgetting justice or perfect justice by forgoing peace.

Nothing is more difficult than defining God. By definition God is infinite and we are not. Any single-minded definition falls short. If God is our friend, God is also the Lord of hosts. If God is close to us, God is also far from us. These two pictures of God, crude as they are, must both inform our faith.

On the other hand, maybe I chose Michael Jordan because he is arguably the best basketball player that ever floated above the court.

# Why I Don't Eat Much Broccoli

Like most mothers mine told me to eat my broccoli, and reminded me that there were hungry people in the world. As I remember it was the Armenians who were starving because I didn't clean my plate. I suppose it is the people of the sub-Sahara or Bangladesh now.

I would gladly have let the Armenians have my broccoli, but that argument didn't get me very far. I quickly learned though that if I ate unattractive vegetables quickly I would get more. I became skillful at eating at just the right speed: fast enough to avoid punishment but slow enough to escape second helpings.

I suppose I would be healthier today if I had eaten more of that broccoli. Our main problem though is not just that we eat the wrong things, but that we eat too much of everything. There is an epidemic of obesity. You only have to look around (or maybe look in a mirror) to see that it is true. There are a lot of fat people around.

In the 18th century the Reverend Thomas Malthus noted with horror that the world population was growing. Malthus predicted that unless this growth was checked people would outstrip the food supply and we would starve. This should be a warning to all clergy not to predict the future.

Malthus was right about population growth. There are more people now than when he wrote. The result however is not starvation. Food production has grown even faster than the population. From rice paddies in the Orient to cornfields in Illinois, we produce more food from less land with fewer farmers than ever before.

Food is more plentiful and less expensive than at any time in history. Where there is hunger it is not because we are running out of food. It is because that we are better at producing food than at distributing it. Hunger is a political problem, not a production problem.

Malthus scared people with the wrong threat. The danger is not that we will run out of food. It is that we will eat more than we should and give less than we ought. Gluttony is a sin. Generosity is not.

# Everybody Has an Opinion

The other day I heard a coach speak. When he was introduced the audience was invited to ask questions "or make suggestions." The coach, a brave man, did not flinch when he heard this. Coaches get a lot of suggestions.

Coaching is one of the professions that attract opinions from just about everyone. Everybody who buys a ticket to a game or contributes to an athletic fund feels qualified to advise the coach. They don't understand that paying money doesn't make you a coach. Somebody has to want to pay you. Then you're a coach.

Most people who give advice think they want to be helpful. Most people who are offered advice don't want that kind of help. Giving advice without being asked is an aggressive act. It asserts superiority over the person advised. It is the claim that you know more than they do. This will not make you popular.

Most mischievous of all are the people who insist on telling people things "for their own good." Wrapped in righteousness, they say gladly what kindness would leave unsaid. It is no defense that what they say is true. Honest people tell the truth. That is good, but it is not the highest good. Caring people tell the truth when it is helpful. They are kind enough to be silent when truth hurts and cannot help.

Some churches have signs outside that carry a message to people passing by. The messages are short, only five or six words. I have great respect for brevity, and I am always interested in what someone will say when they have only a short space to say something important. Last week I saw one that I thought about for several days. It read "God hears prayer, not advice."

Prayer is more than telling God what we would do if we were God. What God actually does is often quite different. That doesn't mean our prayer wasn't heard. Most of the really wonderful things in my life were gifts far better than my prayers. The things I dreaded most were not endless tragedies. God didn't need my advice. The plans of God are richer than the dreams we dream.

# An Ozark Mountain Town

Eureka Springs is an Ozark mountain town. It was founded when Victoria was Queen of England and never got over it. The overblown architecture of the late 19th century still lines its steep, crooked streets. Eureka Springs is a museum that preserves the sights and scenes of a spa in 1876.

It is an unlikely place to build a town. It is on a steep mountain side, its few streets twisting and turning or plunging at improbable angles. There are oddities, like a church that can be entered through the top of its belfry, and a seven story hotel where each floor has a ground floor entrance.

There aren't many places where the past lives on like this. It takes a very special history to make such a place. It has to have a period of prosperity, when impressive buildings are constructed. This must be followed by a long, slow decline

That's what happened in Eureka Springs. In its heyday the railroad brought visitors to drink the waters. Hotels were built to house them, restaurants to feed them, shops to amuse them, and churches to sustain them. The streets were crowded with carriages, bearing stylish visitors to the bath houses and entertainments.

Then spas went out of style. Doctors prescribed medicines, not rest and therapeutic springs. People no longer traveled on railroads. The customers slowly ebbed away, not all at once, but little by little.

It was a delicate balance. If the town had become too poor people would have moved away. The stately buildings would have been abandoned and vandalized. If it had thrived the Victorian hotels would have been replaced by motel chains and the shops by super stores. Neither thing happened. The town simply survived, barely but surely.

Now the streets are busy again, but with tour buses and motor homes instead of carriages. The elegantly attired men and ladies with white gloves and feathered hats are gone. Today's visitors favor shorts and jeans. They come to see the past, not to relive it.

It is important to know about the past, to know where we came from. It is equally important to know that we can't return to it.

# Identity and Passwords

Small boys sometimes form secret clubs. Just what is secret or why it should be is not altogether clear. It was in one such boyish gang that I first learned about passwords. We built a clubhouse out of scraps of plywood. We had a password to keep unauthorized persons out of our clubhouse. We never found out if it would work. No unauthorized person ever wanted in.

When our children were small we had a family password. It was "swordfish." We borrowed it from an old Marx Brothers movie. It had no real purpose. It was just a family joke. Since our children had never seen a Marx Brothers movie they didn't get the joke. They just assumed that their parents were eccentric.

Now everybody uses passwords. Computers demand them frequently. At last count I had 26 passwords I use in different ways. Some I was allowed to choose. I picked passwords that I might remember but probably won't. Others were assigned to me. Those are such a mixture of letters and numbers that no one could remember them.

If you can't give the right password when one is demanded you're in trouble. Guessing is not a good idea. Too many wrong guesses and sometimes your account is locked up. It can only be opened by an act of Congress or with the permission of a senior executive who is usually on vacation.

If you forget your passwords some sites will demand your answer to a secret question you have agreed on. That's easy. You tell them your mother's maiden name or the make of the first car you owned. Others will send you the forgotten countersign by e-mail. Either way, it takes time to straighten out the confusion.

We do all this to prove that we are who we say we are. It protects us from strangers who want to charge things to our credit cards. In cyberspace anybody can use your name. Passwords keep strangers from claiming to be you in expensive ways.

You need a password for every important transaction except one. You don't need a password for your prayers. God knows who you are, better than you know yourself.

# Are We Almost There?

Driving on an Interstate highway is a lot like flying. In both cases you leave one place and arrive at another without being anywhere in between. The joy is not in the journey. It is in arriving. What lies between is boredom and discomfort. The main differences are that the plane gets you there quicker but it costs more.

Some Interstate highways go through places that are beautiful. You may never notice the scenery. Nature's beauty is hard to appreciate at 70 miles an hour with a slow semi-trailer in front of you, a fast one passing you, and another closing rapidly from behind. The clouds you see when you're flying are beautiful too, but they get monotonous. One cloud is a lot like another.

When travel becomes boring we are tempted to take a nap. Sleeping is not advisable while driving a car. It is essential to have a companion who will help you stay awake. The companion will promptly fall asleep. Keeping the companion awake will make you too nervous to sleep.

It is possible to sleep on a plane if you are very rich or very small. If you have enough money or Frequent Flyer Points you can fly First Class or Business Class. If you are small enough you can sleep comfortably in coach. Everyone else is wedged into seats designed for interviewing critics of the beloved leader in a third-rate dictatorship. Forcing prisoners to fly coach is probably a violation of the Geneva Convention.

If you are traveling with children, shortly after the plane takes off or just as the car backs out of the driveway somebody will ask "Are we almost there?" This is a perfectly reasonable question. Getting to the destination is the only thing there is to look forward to. What happens until then is just filling dead time.

We may not have much choice about the way we travel, but we can decide where we will go. The destination is the important decision. If we are going to the right place it doesn't matter how we get there. That's true of family vacations. It is just as true of your goals in life.

# Violence and Little League Sports

Most people think there are four seasons, but for some there are only three. They are football, basketball, and baseball. Anything else is just off-season training.

A few people play these sports, but many more watch. That's why there are stadiums and arenas that seat tens of thousands of spectators. There are few experiences more pleasant than a summer afternoon at Wrigley Field or a fall Saturday at a Big Ten stadium. If your team wins it's a perfect day. Even losing is better than missing the game.

Unlike European soccer fans, Americans don't riot at ball games. That isn't because we don't care about our teams. We just don't have a tradition of hooliganism at sporting events. Instead we have a mantra we chant when our team loses. It is "Wait 'till next year." It is possible to say this every year for decades. It has been done. It represents the triumph of hope over experience.

One reason we don't attack the other team when we lose is that we have a better way of dealing with disappointment. We fire the coach. A coach who has repeated winning seasons only raises expectations. At some traditional power house schools a coach is in jeopardy if he wins by too narrow a margin. One loss and he has to buy his own shoes.

The one place in American sports where passions may get out of hand is in children's leagues. The kids are usually well behaved, but sometimes their parents aren't. They may have trouble dealing with disappointment. They can't even fire the coach. Somebody might ask them to take his place.

If players are abusive to the officials they can be tossed out of the game. The players are smaller than the officials. Their parents aren't. On the whole, some children's leagues would be a better example of behavior if the parents played and the kids cheered.

There are two points of view about winning in sports. One is that winning is the most important thing. The other is that winning is the only thing. If losing builds character, we are big enough to let the other team have the benefit of it.

# Lady Bug Explosion

Thanks to the Internet we can find out a lot about almost anything very quickly. That's how I know so much about ladybugs.

There seems to be a population explosion of ladybugs going on. I've seen a lot of them lately, mostly in my car. They don't swarm in great crowds. They appear one at a time. They walk across my windshield, they stroll along the dash, they climb up the windows.

If we have to have insects, ladybugs are the kind to have. They don't bite or sting, they don't carry diseases, and they don't damage crops. They aren't ugly. In fact, a ladybug is sort of cute, rather like a tiny Volkswagen. They are even useful. Ladybugs eat aphids, which do damage crops. Farmers sometimes buy ladybugs by the gallon to protect their crops. There are about 75,000 ladybugs in a gallon.

There are a lot of different ladybug breeds. There are 400 kinds in North America alone. There are two-spotted, five-spotted, and fifteen-spotted ladybugs. There are even eye-spotted ladybugs, whose spots look like tiny eyes. These distinctions are of interest only to other ladybugs.

Many people think ladybugs are good luck. I am told that in Sweden some believe that if a ladybug lands on a young maiden's head she will get married soon. That's probably true. If a ladybug doesn't land on a young maiden's head she will still probably get married soon. That's what young maidens do.

I know all these things about ladybugs because the little fellows have a web site. All the candidates for President have web sites. Everybody who wants to be governor of California has a web site. Fortunately ladybugs don't care about this. They just go on munching aphids. Ladybugs have no known political tendencies.

# Geese, Go Home to Canada!

The Canada Goose is a migratory bird. They used to go north to Canada in the summer and south to Florida in the winter, rather like retired physicians. We saw them twice a year as they passed through. We enjoyed their brief visits.

Their visits aren't so brief any more. They have become suburbanites. They have given up their northern lakes and settled for the ponds created by real estate developers. I don't know how the geese feel about this, but I think it is a very bad idea.

In flight they are magnificent, awesome as they cross the sky in orderly V formation. They gracefully wheel and honk, masters of their heavenly universe. As long as they stay in the sky we can admire them and be grateful for the sight.

On the ground they aren't so good. Their dignity is compromised by their graceless manner of walking. They waddle around like a chorus of drunken bishops. Their personal hygiene is lamentable. They are pretty in the sky but ugly on your lawn. The better we know them, the less we like them.

This contradicts the common notion that if people know each other they will like each other. Having an intimate relationship with geese will not make you love birds. It will make you hate the smell of your back yard.

People used to eat geese. It was the main dish on holidays. You can't eat these geese. Migratory birds are protected. You can't touch them. Put one of these buzzards on your back yard grill and the feds will take you away in handcuffs.

This raises an important question. How do you live with a creature you can't love, can't escape, and can't eat?

When I was a seminary student there was a professor who counseled young seminarians having their first experience of rural churches. When a student reported some particularly irrational act of a church board the professor always said the same thing: "You'll just have to love them into being better."

We were convinced that the man was an idiot. It didn't work any better with Presbyterian farmers than with Canada geese. Some things you just have to put up with.

# Subject to Cancellation

I've had my new car for a couple of months and I really like it. I didn't mind what it cost because it's probably the last car I'll ever buy. I think it's a beautiful car.

Once I got a lot of enjoyment from my work and from the children in our family. Now my children are grown and my career is long over. A new car is one of the few things that still give me pleasure.

All of that pleasure stopped suddenly on a Saturday afternoon. It happened on a street corner. The light was green for me, but the young woman for whom it was red didn't see it. We've all had moments when our mind wandered while we were driving. Hers wandered that afternoon and she didn't stop for the light.

We met loudly in the intersection. My car wasn't so pretty then. I felt sad.

That's pretty pathetic. Why should I feel sad? It is shameful to stake my happiness on an automobile. There couldn't be a clearer case of something that "moth and rust will corrupt and thieves break in to steal."

Everybody else responded better than I did. The young woman whose momentary inattention caused the accident hurried to my car. She was mainly concerned that one of us might be hurt. (We weren't.) The accident was an inconvenience for me. For her it was a problem and an expense she hadn't expected, yet she was concerned for us.

A passing truck driver phoned the police, and then got out of his truck to be helpful. He picked up the pieces of my car from the street. Later her insurance company acted like a good neighbor, quickly authorizing repairs and a rental car. The company that rented me a car offered the best they had. It proved to be a red mini-van, the soccer-mom's home away from home.

I'll enjoy the car again when it has been repaired. But I won't count on it to make me happy. Like all earthly pleasures it is perishable. It is like a cheap airline ticket: good for this day and this flight only, and subject to cancellation without notice.

# Bee Line Expressway

The Bee Line Expressway is a toll road leading to Orlando, Florida. Near the International Airport there is a toll station, a line of eight booths where a steady stream of motorists hand over a dollar and a quarter.

A lot of money passes through those toll booths every day. It's the kind of taxation politicians dream about. The amount each person pays is too small to upset anybody, but so many people are taxed that it produces a whole lot of money.

That's why entertainers and athletes are better paid than plumbers or brain surgeons. Plumbers can only work on one house at a time and brain surgeons treat a handful of patients. An arena full of fans can produce the big bucks without anyone paying all that much.

There's a big difference in what you are getting for your money, of course. Both the plumber and the surgeon must give their full attention to you. The entertainer doesn't even know who you are.

Entertainers are paid to entertain crowded venues. That's okay. You don't mind sharing your entertainment with thousands of others. You just don't want to have your plumbing or your brain treated that way.

That's one of the basic contradictions of modern life. The world progresses by becoming increasingly efficient, and efficiency demands that life be more and more impersonal. Our ancestors went to one-room schools and shopped at the neighborhood store. Stores have become bigger; schools are larger, churches are morphing into mega-churches.

The butcher used to cut our steaks and chops exactly as we wanted them, and ask about our relatives as he did it. Nobody even sees a butcher any more. The butchers are all cutting meat in some hidden meat-cutting factory. They don't know your relatives.

We live a lot better than our ancestors did. In this efficient age we can afford more meat, fancier houses, and better schools. We just wish someone would know who we are.

Faith is our one refuge from the mass market. We confess our own sins, not the sins of mankind. We are forgiven individually, not in a crowd. God knows exactly who you are. That's good.

# Peter Pan Was Right

Grandchildren are great, except for one thing. If you have them you are a grandparent. I don't think anyone looks forward to that. Grandparents are old, and nobody wants to be old.

Peter Pan, who wanted to stay a child forever, had the right idea. He just quit too early. Most children sensibly want to grow up as quickly as possible. They want to stay up late and sleep late and wear all the clothes their parents hate. Adolescents want to grow up so they can express their individuality. They do this by dressing, talking, and thinking exactly like everyone else their age.

When we become adults there are a lot of first things: first job, first house, first car, and first child. There is a first family vacation and a first promotion. We look forward to getting past all those firsts into a settled, normal life.

We get past the firsts by becoming middle aged. Middle age can be any age. For some it doesn't come until they're fifty-five, although that doesn't mean they'll live to be a hundred and ten. Some are middle aged before they're thirty, and a few appear to be born middle aged. Middle age is the time when many things are pleasant but nothing is exciting. It is when you know you're not ever going to be rich, famous, and beautiful, but you don't envy those who are.

After that the refrigerator wears out, the dog dies, and the kids get married. That's probably the age Peter Pan should have tried to hold on to. For a few days you are peaceful, unstressed, and contented. You are not driven by the fires of ambition or the terrors of responsibility. Very few things trouble you. You have forgiven your enemies and accepted your limitations. Life is good.

Then your doctor starts talking about "the aging process" and your friends begin to look old. That's when God gives us grandchildren. They're too busy to pay a lot of attention to us, but we always have time to enjoy them. Most of the time they're a lot of fun, and when they're not we can always send them home to their parents.

# Unremarkable

Some words mean different things at different times. It depends on who says them and when. If a teacher says a student is "unremarkable" that's bad news. Not much hope of a scholarship there, you think. If your doctor says the result of your test is unremarkable, that's good news. There are times when you don't want to stand out. You want a mediocre cat scan, not one that inspires an article in a medical journal.

People don't usually aspire to mediocrity, but being middle class isn't bad. The country needs middle class people. A large middle class is necessary for a democracy. Neither poverty nor riches make people want freedom. The poor want a country that will help them and the wealthy want a country that will leave them alone. It is the many who are neither rich nor poor who benefit from democracy. It is the middle class who will create, defend, and expand democratic government.

There are outstanding people who change the course of history. They make great discoveries; create beauty that is timeless. Their brilliance lights up the time in which they live. Einstein and Beethoven, Magellan and Shakespeare – their genius turned the world in a different course than it would otherwise have followed. We all benefit from their genius.

The world only needs an occasional genius, a few in every century. It needs a lot of competent, noble, ordinary people. I suppose I owe a debt to the genius who invented the wheel. I know I owe one to the factory workers who made the wheels on which I ride. Genius is wonderful, but it's the middle class that makes the world go around.

Middle class people do ordinary things in an extraordinary way. They care about their work and they do it as well as it can be done. They don't cure diseases, but they give loving care to the people who struggle with them. They don't create great art or music, but they produce the food that supports those who do.

We honor spiritual giants by calling them saints. But there are middle class saints for whom no churches are named. We don't know their names. God does.

# Neither Stupid Nor Evil, But Wrong

There are people in the world who hate us and want to kill us. They want to kill us because we are Americans. That is a hard fact to accept, but a dangerous one to ignore.

Sometimes I have a moment of brilliant inspiration. Suddenly complicated things seem very simple, and I understand questions that have puzzled me for a long time. It's like a light being turned on in the darkness.

I've learned from experience not to trust these inspirations. They are almost always dead wrong. When things seem complicated to me, it is usually because they are. When they seem simple, I'm on the wrong track.

There are people whose convictions are very clear to them. They know what they believe. They are sure that everyone should think as they do. They ought to be suspicious of their certainty.

They may be vegetarians or pacifists or belong to a mainline church or an online sect. They may be democrats or republicans or Zoroastrians. Their faith is really quite simple. They believe that they are right. They are true believers.

True believers think that any sensible person will agree with them if they can only be made to understand. If they explain their cause slowly and clearly people will recognize the logic of their position. They are likely to keep explaining over and over again if you don't agree. Anyone who doesn't agree is either stupid or evil. True believers are not a lot of fun to be with.

If you think this way there are only three kinds of people in the world: people exactly like yourself, foolish people, and monsters of evil. This limits your social life. It may cripple your moral life.

There are people who are neither stupid nor evil who yet are wrong. They are not bad people who should be exterminated or slow minded people who can be convinced. They have made a choice, and it is the wrong choice.

If everyone knew that the world would be a better place. People could believe and disagree passionately without feeling the need to murder anyone. Our belief would make us kinder, and not lead us to commit horrors.

# A Boy from Italy

There were two new students in my class the last year I was a student at McKinley Grade School in Kokomo, Indiana. One was Egidio, who was Italian and spoke very little English. His parents came to Indiana to escape from the Italian dictator, Mussolini.

We assumed that Egidio was stupid because he couldn't speak English well. This was a mistake.

Some of the boys tried to teach Egidio some shocking four letter words, hoping he would startle the teacher. At first Egidio pretended not to hear well, making them repeat the words over and over. Finally he asked Jim, his chief tormenter, to write the words down. When Jim obliged Egidio took the paper to the teacher, asking haltingly for help in pronouncing the words Jim was teaching him. No one thought Egidio was stupid after that.

Then there was Billy, whose family moved to town in the middle of the year. Billy was the boy every parent wishes their son would be. He was the Boy Scout Law incarnate: trustworthy, loyal, helpful and all the rest. He said "please" and "thank you" and "M'am" and "Sir" without fail. He participated in sports, did homework for extra credit, and never, ever told a lie. His hair was always combed, his clothes were always neat, and dirt did not stick to him.

The kids all hated Billy.

We hated Billy not because he was good, but because he was publicly good. He tried very hard to be seen to be better than us. He wanted everyone to appreciate his goodness. It was his goal in life.

Not everyone who claims to be moral is more moral than others. Consider all the different people who say they want peace. The implication is not only that they want peace, but that everyone else prefers violence. The really difficult question is not who wants peace, but how we can keep the peace in a warlike world. There is plenty of room for disagreement about that.

Many people want to claim the high moral ground, particularly in an election year. In fact, the high moral ground is very crowded this year. Sometimes what seems like virtue is only boasting.

# The Good Lives On

Where does the time go? Another year is ending. As we get older the annual holidays come closer together. They rush by, almost falling over one another, like children escaping from school.

There are several New Year's Days. The Chinese have a different New Year, and so do Jews. In our part of the world we use the Gregorian calendar, but before that there was a Julian calendar. Changing from one to the other changed the New Year. There are fiscal years and tax years, all of which start at some time. There was a Mayan calendar in ancient Mexico, so important that it was laboriously carved in stone. Just about everybody has had some way to measure the passing of time.

Civilized society is impossible without a calendar. We need to know when to pay our taxes, and when a person is old enough to vote, drive a car, or run for Congress. To buy a house we need a mortgage, to pay a mortgage we need a calendar.

Sometimes time goes by quickly, sometimes it creeps by on leaden feet. When we were young a semester lasted forever, except near the end when papers came due. Then it speeded up and so did we. Or maybe we didn't.

We can measure time, but we can't control it. We can't speed it up or slow it down. We can't make good times last forever. We can remember the happiest days in our life but we can't return to them. We can regret some things we have done but we can't undo them. We can't change the past, but the past surely changes us.

Only one thing can change the past: forgiveness. Even forgiveness doesn't undo what was done. It doesn't remove the effects of what we have done. The forgiven prisoner must still serve his sentence. Forgiveness frees us from being what our past would make us. It changes what we have made ourselves.

The good we do in life lives on. It is still good. The rest can be forgiven. We don't have to repeat it or be changed by it. That's the good news at the beginning of another year.

# Aunt Lora's Treasures

When Aunt Lora died we found drawers filled with Christmas gifts. Each bore a tag that told who had given it to her, the year they gave it, and the date on which she wrote a thank-you note. None of the gifts had ever been used.

She was a sweet, kind-hearted lady, and she would not for the world have wanted anyone to know that she didn't use their gifts. She was always effusively grateful. But the fact remained that it wasn't the gifts for which she was grateful. She was grateful that we wanted to give them to her.

She had reached a time in her life when she didn't have much but she didn't want more. No one could give her the only things she lacked. Her beloved Homer died long before she did. To have him alive and by her side would be a gift worth her longing. We couldn't give her that.

Next to Uncle Homer her most prized gift was her memories. She loved to remember when relatives now grown had been babies. Sometimes she embarrassed them by remembering too well. Young adults are not pleased to have stories about their potty training recounted to their peers.

No one had to give these memories to her. No one could take them away. She talked about those memories as though they were yesterday, when often they happened years ago.

Lora and Homer had no children of their own. Nephews and nieces filled the empty space in their hearts. Those nephews and nieces were specially blessed. It was like having another set of grandparents.

Their life was simple, uncomplicated, and happy. They had nothing to give but love. They asked nothing except to be loved in return. Kings and queens were not as rich as they were.

What they illustrated was unconditional love, the kind of love that suffers all things, enjoys all things, and asks nothing in return. It is love that is sometimes disappointed but never gives up. It is love that celebrates the best and applauds it. It is love that sees the worst and grieves

Some theologians claim that God loves us that way. I hope they're right.

# The Idiot We Almost Married

People who live in the north sometimes say they don't want to move to a warmer climate because they would miss seeing the seasons change. The seasons change a lot in Illinois. Sometimes they change several times in one week.

The changeable weather makes winter travel a little uncertain. We don't always arrive when we plan to arrive. Flights are delayed and sometimes cancelled. Roads become icy and hazardous. Usually this is no more than an annoyance. It calls on us to have patience. We may arrive late, but we will arrive.

Our changeable weather is good for our souls. It reminds us that we aren't in control of the world. No matter how carefully we plan we will sometimes be surprised. Success doesn't always come from good plans. It is just as important to deal successfully with plans that fail.

Peter Marshall, a popular Scottish pastor, is reported to have looked at an unattractive meal of tired leftovers. He sighed and said he didn't think he could give thanks for it. There are days like that for all of us. We plan for sirloin and get cold, greasy meat loaf.

When Plan B is the only choice we have it doesn't help to complain about it. Reality doesn't adapt to our wishes. We have to do the adapting. Success in life is partly a matter of having the right goals and persisting until we reach them. It is just as much a matter of making the best of bad situations.

Sometimes the unwanted situation turns out to be the best one. It takes time and perspective to see that. More than one young heart has been broken over a relationship that deserved to fail. More than one middle aged person has looked back and been thankful that they were prevented from marrying an idiot who seemed attractive at the time.

We pray "Thy will be done," but often God's will is quite different from what we want. The purpose of prayer is not to make God do what we want. It is to inspire us to want what God gives, knowing that it is better than our earth-bound wishes.

# Voyagers in the Same Lifeboat

My mother-in-law, who is in her 93$^{rd}$ year, lives in a retirement home in Florida. It is her home in the best sense of the word. It is the place she is always glad to come back to, the place where her favorite things are all around her.

This spring she was in a hospital for several weeks. I have never met anyone who liked being in a hospital. It is nothing like home. Everything around you is unfamiliar, and you probably aren't feeling very well anyway or you wouldn't be there.

Every night my mother-in-law got a phone call just before she went to sleep. She slept better because of it. The caller even came to visit her. That wasn't easy to do. She had to get the help of her daughter to bring her and push her wheel chair. Her friend is 97.

When my mother-in-law was discharged from the hospital I drove her home. I stayed to have lunch with her. As the other residents filed into the dining room dozens of them came over to her table, one at a time. They beamed a smiling welcome, told her how glad they were to see her back. There was warmth and laughter and good natured chatter about the indignities of aging.

I thought I was a caregiver. I realized then that I was only one of many caregivers. She was surrounded by people who cared about her and supported her. Among the saddest words in the English language is the word "alone." She was not alone.

These caregivers understood what she was going through in ways that I don't. They feared what she feared; the same rapidly approaching future loomed over them. They were united by the experiences they shared.

My mother-in-law and her friends were voyagers in the same lifeboat. They were lifted by the same swells, drenched by the same waves. They had the same hope of rescue, and the same discomforts and fears. I could sympathize. They could understand.

"I will be with you always," says the Bible, "even if you go to the ends of the earth." Sometimes God sends someone to keep that promise.

# A Stranger in the Mirror

A young woman once said to me, "I don't know who I am."

I gave her a standard seminary textbook response and waited for her to tell me why she said this.

"You're the child of God. Maybe an adolescent child, rebellious and not on very good terms with your parents, but you're still family."

I didn't say anything about her glasses. I've been thinking about glasses and identity lately.

I used to be near-sighted, but I'm not any more. I wasn't healed miraculously. A few years ago cataracts were removed from my eyes and the clouded lenses replaced with prescription implants.

After that my vision was near perfect. However I still need correction for reading. I've continued wearing bifocal spectacles.

Last week my optometrist suggested I get some simple magnifying glasses at a drug store and not wear glasses when I don't need them. He recommended two pairs: one for reading and the other for looking at a computer screen. They work fine, except for one thing.

I can't get used to not wearing glasses. They have been part of me since I was an adolescent Harry Potter look-alike. Without glasses I feel undressed, which is a distinctly uncomfortable feeling in public places.

I am used to seeing myself with glasses. Now I see a stranger in the mirror. A friend I've known for years looked at me with a vaguely puzzled expression. She shook her head as though she were clearing away cobwebs and said, "For a minute I didn't know who you were. I don't know why." I knew why.

I am surprised to find that my glasses, which I have never thought about much one way or another, are part of my identity. If someone asks who I am, I would never say, "I'm a man who wears glasses."

I've changed in lots of more important ways. I am taller than when I was a child. I am wider than when I retired. None of those changes made me feel like a different person.

I'm still the child of God, maybe a rebellious, adolescent child, and nothing changes that. Still, I think I might just keep on wearing my glasses.

# The Great Leader is a Great Lie

The political season is upon us again. It is an essential part of democracy but it is not a pretty thing to see. Promises are being made that will never be kept. Incumbents point with pride to their accomplishments. Those who hope to replace them view the same record with alarm. Pointing with pride and viewing with alarm is what politicians do.

A congressman once told me that if we chose our national leaders at random with a computer we would have exactly the same kind of people as those we elect. Many are wise and a few are fools, some have high standards for their own life and others have little or none. We choose people no better or worse than we are. They appeal to our noblest virtues and our most grievous faults. We answer both appeals. In a democracy, we get the government we deserve.

It is an imperfect system, but there is no better one available to us. We are imperfect people. The best we can hope for is that our government will be pretty good, just as we are pretty good. Not perfect, just pretty good. Sometimes we don't even get that, just as sometimes we aren't quite good.

In a democratic country the people who lose an election aren't killed. That is very important. The losers stay around and criticize the winners. Like good Chicago Cub fans their mantra is "Wait until next year." If the electorate made a mistake, there will soon be a chance to correct it.

Totalitarian societies are built on the belief that there is one perfect person. The Great Leader is without fault and beyond reproach. Democratic societies are based on the belief that there is no such person. The Great Leader is a Great Lie.

Democracy works because it is realistic about who we are. We are all made in the image of God, capable of caring for the weak and helpless, able to love and be loved. We all fall short of what we are meant to be, capable of corruption and fear.

Every time we vote we should pray. Voting is an act of faith.

# Betrayed by Our Own Technology

When I was in college I had an old car. It served me quite well, but only if I humored it. It had an automatic choke that wasn't automatic. To start it I had to raise the hood, push the choke down and wedge it with an old rag. After I started the engine I had to rush outside, pull the rag free, slam the hood, and dash back behind the wheel. People stared at me when I started my car in public places.

Now I am humoring an old telephone. If I answer it before it rings twice it sighs and hangs up. It also doesn't like call waiting. When a caller tries to put me on hold it breaks the connection. When a caller says they have another call I desperately rush to another phone, crying "Wait! Wait!" Most people think this is a little strange.

Cars and telephones are old technology. Today we are betrayed by more sophisticated devices. That doesn't mean they are more reliable. What it does mean is that when a computer or a DVD player starts doing strange things we have no idea what is wrong or what we can do to live with it. The technology that lets us do things we never dreamed lures us into frustrations beyond our nightmares.

This is not a new problem. In Stockholm there is a museum that houses a warship named the Vasa. It was built in 1628, the most advanced ship of its time. When it was launched crowds lined the shore to watch this technological marvel.

The crowds gasped when the ship started across the harbor, leaned far to one side, turned over, and sank. The crew went with it. The Vasa remained on the bottom of the harbor until 1961, when it was raised and installed in its museum.

Technology is good. I like my computers and my car and my PDA. But they are a lot like me. When they are good they are very good, but they aren't always good.

That's why the basic questions of faith are "Can I be forgiven? Who can help me live like I was meant to live?"

# Big Days Pass Swiftly

Last week we came home after a long absence. Almost as soon as we got back we went to a wedding. It was a happy ending to the trip. Weddings are a lot of fun. Seeing the happiness of someone we know makes us happy.

Sometimes happiness takes us by surprise, but usually we have to work for it. Most good things can be enjoyed three times: once when they are being planned, again when they happen, and finally when they are remembered. That is true of weddings, vacations, and commencements. It is also true of moving to a new home, having a baby, and starting a job. The Big Day is important, but it is only one part of the joy. Happiness stretches out in both directions.

Being able to dream and to remember are two of the richest gifts of being human. I don't know whether animals dream or not, and it's not clear how much pleasure they have in remembering. What is clear is that we get a lot of happiness from both dreams and memories.

Dreams don't always come true. We plan trips we never take, and hope for more than we can realize. If dreams do happen the reality may be quite different from what we expected. That takes nothing away from the joy of the moment. The only thing worse than a failed dream is never having dreamed at all.

All the Big Days in our life pass swiftly. We wish the joy could last forever. Instead it is over almost before we know it. That's why we celebrate anniversaries and birthdays, buy cameras and recorders, and have reunions and make scrapbooks. We want to live the happy time again and again, and make it last a long time, if not forever.

When we dream and when we remember we break free from the tyranny of time. We are not trapped in the present, like flies in a spider web. We can hope for what lies ahead and cherish what is behind us. The saddest question about life is, "Is this all there is?"

The answer is "No. There is more. Life stretches out into eternity."

# Fighting a Battle We Can't Win

My doctor, who is a kindly man, did not tell me I was fat. He gave me a chart relating weight to height, with a circle around the word, "obese." He suggested I hang it up above my scale.

For my sins at the dinner table I exercise daily. I am not alone at the fitness center. The parking lot is full all day. Weight control is where the action is in popular medicine today. Smoking has been defeated, its loyalists shamed and banned from contact with others. Just about everybody is having their colonoscopy and mammogram on the approved schedule. Combating obesity is the cause du jour.

There are two kinds of people on the treadmills and bicycles of fitness centers. Some are young, healthy, and beautiful. They talk about pects and abs, lift great weights, and bounce from one machine to the next. I try not to look at them.

The rest aren't trying to perfect their bodies. They just want to keep them working a little longer. They talk about carbs and calories and read books that promise a lot more than they deliver. They are important to the national economy. Weight loss is a major industry, and they are its customers.

Losing weight is expensive. Those foods with carbohydrates counted cost more than ordinary eats. Personal trainers and group pep sessions aren't free. In other countries the poor are thin and look hungry. Here it takes money to be thin and look hungry. Poor people can't afford it.

The irony of this is that we are fighting a battle we can't win. We will all grow old, our bodies will become unlovely, and in time we will die. We can slow the aging process, but only a little. Mostly we just disguise it, with flesh toned and tanned and wrinkles ironed out with injections or surgery. For all our effort, our bodies still grow old. We will never be twenty again.

Our flesh ages but our spirits mature. We have more to gain from developing our souls than our bodies. Learning how to count carbohydrates may make you better for a year or two. Learning to pray will make you better forever.

# If God Is In Control, Where Is He Taking Us?

There are bridges in Europe that have lasted for centuries. The same bridges I saw a half century ago still span the Seine or the Thames. For some reason many of ours seem to be wearing out this year. Bridges are being repaired or replaced on interstate highways, county roads, and even city streets. Detours and work zones interrupt every trip, short or long.

A lot of our bridges are still good, but they aren't as wide as we need. We are a mobile people. Our trucks get bigger, and there are more cars every year. Lanes are added to highways and streets. Wide roads and narrow bridges can be a lethal combination. Correcting that makes a lot of people travel farther and slower than they planned.

People in our hurry-up society don't react kindly to being delayed. A few rebel by refusing to slow down, a decision that can turn suicidal for some and homicidal for others. Many more simply tap their fingers impatiently on the steering wheel and work at brewing up an ulcer. This does not get them where they are going any faster.

Detours and work zones are bad for our plans, but they may be good for our souls. What we dislike most about these interruptions is that there is absolutely nothing we can do about them. We can't control them. We don't like that.

It does us good to be reminded of how little we can control. From our first living breath we have been blessed or cursed by things we didn't choose and can't change. We didn't control the choice of our parents and our nationality at the beginning of our life.

At the end of life we don't control the day or the manner of our dying. In the years between we are continually being slowed in our progress or stopped and sent in a new direction. Some things we can plan. Many we must simply accept. It is better if we accept them graciously.

To say that God is in control is only half an answer. The remaining question is whether the detour is a blessing or simply a nuisance. I vote for blessing.

# The Best Laid Plans Go Astray

Sometimes we make good plans, prepare for them carefully, and then see them go completely wrong.

The Relay for Life is a fund raising event of the American Cancer Society. The format is simple. People whose lives have been touched by cancer (which includes almost everybody) form teams. They give money and collect money from others. Team members take turns walking around a track through all the night hours. There is music, food, and a few short speeches.

Because I was away from home on the critical week-end I joined a team in Evanston, Illinois. It was held at a high school sports field. The teams had been recruited, the contributions had been gathered, and tents and canopies surrounded the track.

Musicians played earnestly. The mayor made a speech; the cancer survivors led the way, first to walk the circuit. You could smell the brats and burgers cooking on the grill. I sat comfortably under a canopy. A local radio personality narrated the festivities. It was a perfect event.

Then everything came unraveled. "Relay for Life" became "Run for Your Life."

The narrator said in an off-hand way, "There are reports that there might be a little wind, so take care of your newspapers and magazines."

Within seconds a howling gale swept through. The canopy under which I sat rose in the air, overturned a neighboring tent, and knocked a woman to the ground. The empty chair beside me became airborne. Everyone was snatching objects large and small that hurtled through the air. Dark rain clouds advanced from the West.

That was the end of the Relay. Participants hurriedly gathered their belongings and fled to their cars before the deluge began. The people who worked so hard for the Relay presided over an entirely different event than they expected.

It wasn't really a disaster, though. The money had already been collected, so the purpose was fulfilled. Some people who had promised to walk in the small hours of the morning were home in their own beds instead. Best of all, it will be remembered longer than most charitable events.

Faith doesn't make God do what we want. It makes us want what God does.

# Faith Makes Us Ask Hard Questions

Ronald Reagan has died. It was a long, sad death; mercifully out of sight of all but his family and a few others. The White House has housed three other families since the Reagans left it. With his passing we are reminded of an earlier day, when our fears and hopes were different.

Both his friends and his enemies acknowledge that the world was changed by Reagan's presidency. Most would say that he more than anyone else changed it. Marxism, once hailed as the wave of the future, is now only a sad aberration of the past. Democracy, which was in retreat, has greatly expanded.

Today we live in fear of terrorists. Then we lived in the shadow of Mutually Assured Destruction. (Does anyone remember when children huddled under school desks in nuclear attack drills and church basements were stocked with survival foods and cans of water?) The more things change, the more they are the same.

Both Reagan's supporters and his critics are much older now. There are voters today who were born after Reagan's first term began. For the most part the aging journalists and politicians of that era have not changed their views. The few who supported the former president salute his accomplishments. The many who did everything they could to thwart him are silent or damn him with faint praise.

That is as it should be. The issues that motivated Ronald Reagan are still debated. We are still not agreed whether we should defeat enemies or negotiate with them, whether government power should be enlarged or limited, whether taxes should be higher or lower.

Ronald Reagan did not leave a final answer to these questions. What he did do was make us consider them. Through decades of the Cold War these questions were not asked. Everyone knew the proper answers. Both parties, Republican and Democrat, placed them out of bounds. To ask such things and entertain the possibility that what everyone accepted was wrong was shocking and possibly dangerous.

Faith does not answer the hard questions. It asks them. God gave us the freedom to give the wrong answers. We are not free to refuse to think about them.

# Everyone Travels First Class

Everybody has heard about the Queen Mary 2. It's the biggest cruise ship in the world, at least for the time being. A larger ship is already being built, but all records are made to be broken.

The ship is called Queen Mary 2, not Queen Mary II and certainly not Queen Mary the Second. There is something inescapably British about this distinction. If you ask, they will tell you it is because this is a ship, not a person. To understand why that is an explanation you have to be British.

It is the only trans-Atlantic ocean liner still in regular service. Other ships make trips across the ocean in the spring and fall, setting up shop where the customers are. QM2 shuttles back and forth on a regular schedule for much of each year. It's transportation, not just a sight-seeing excursion.

In fact, there isn't much to see on a QM2 trip. There are no ports between New York and Southampton. One stretch of ocean looks just like the next. The real challenge for such a trip is keeping the passengers from being bored out of their minds while staring at the unchanging sea.

To meet this challenge the QM2 is armed with more equipment for entertainment than for navigation. There are floor shows and movies, piano bars and a casino. There is a spa and a complete fitness center. Lecturers from Oxford and Cambridge educate the passengers. QM2 even has a planetarium to encourage passengers to look at something besides the empty water.

The dining arrangements are a reflection of the class conscious British. It is designed to separate the beautiful people from the merely pretty. There is a small grill for those who travel in suites and an even smaller grill for those in really expensive suites. Ordinary people are watered and fed in two shifts in their own immense eating hall.

You may recall that the Titanic had a similar arrangement. After the ship hit the iceberg the class distinctions didn't matter. People who refused to eat with commoners were obliged to drown with them.

It was almost Biblical. On the road to heaven everybody travels First Class.

# The Unsolved Mystery of Faith

I am often awake in the middle of the night. It takes a while to go back to sleep. Last week in the small hours I heard an owl. At least, I thought it was an owl. I don't know enough about owls to be sure.

Owls in comic strips hoot. What I heard was definitely hooting. It was also in the darkest hours of the night. The songbirds of daytime were all tucked into their nests. Only nighttime predators were about. That would include owls.

My knowledge of owls is pretty much confined to what you can learn from cartoons. I could be wrong. Maybe I was listening to one of the neighborhood cats complain about being a bachelor. I have never heard an amorous cat hoot, but maybe they do. It would be a change from the howls they usually make.

Once your mind begins wandering like this you might as well give up any hope of going back to sleep. Sleep may knit up the raveled sleeve of care, but it is easily defeated by an unraveled mind. The ability to reason is the blessing of being human. The inability to stop reasoning is the curse.

There are times when we need to stop reasoning. The deepest tragedies and the greatest triumphs lie outside the realm of our reason. Wordsworth wrote about "One that would peep and botanize upon his mother's grave." When grief weighs us down we are likely to ask "Why?" We want to make sense of a hurt so deep that there is no sense to it.

It is the wrong question. If we knew the answer we would hurt no less.

In the same way great joy is unreasonable. It is not something we have planned and made. More often we are surprised by it. We frequently   find happiness not when we are looking for it in the right place, but when we aren't looking for it at all. We don't know why we are blessed. If we did, we would be no happier.

That's why there is always an element of mystery in great faith. Faith is not unreasonable, but it does not stop at the limits of reason.

# Everybody Is Welcome, Nobody Is Favored

A Fourth of July parade is a peculiarly American event. There is a great deal of enthusiasm in it and no particular logic. Anyone that wants to can participate. There are no standards; there is no judging, and no unifying theme. It is democracy taking to the streets.

There are bands, of course. Many represent high schools. They learn to suffer for their art. To walk a long distance in blazing heat, more or less in step, and drag along a musical instrument is cruel punishment. I was in a high school band. I played a clarinet, one of the smaller instruments. The bass and baritone horns had a harder time, and so did some of the drummers. I had no sympathy for them. They chose their lot. Still I envied the piccolo players, who could stick their instruments in their pockets.

You can count on a full complement of politicians. Some ride in convertibles, with a sign bearing the name that will appear on the ballot. The younger ones walk, particularly those of a populist persuasion. They stride from one side to the other, leaving no hand unshaken. Sometimes they give things away, like cardboard fans or ball point pens with their name on them. That is so voters will associate their name with generosity.

If it is a really good parade there will be a squad of Shriners. Everybody loves the Shriners. They always ride something: tiny cars, little motor scooters, or anything else they can think of. They maneuver with great precision, doing circles and figure eights. They have a serious purpose in raising money to help crippled children, but there is nothing serious about them in a parade. They are just a bunch of middle-aged men behaving like fools and loving it.

Some groups are in a parade to advertise a business and others to promote a cause. Either one is okay. The parade organizers try to separate competing causes with some uncontroversial 4H kids and a blaring sound truck from a Hard Rock radio station.

Everybody is who wants to come is welcome at a Fourth of July parade, and nobody is favored. Maybe heaven is like that.

# Some People Exploit What Other People Create

My current cell phone can receive text messages. It is a feature I haven't bothered to learn to use. Since the message has to be patiently tapped in from an ordinary telephone keyboard it isn't a very good way to communicate. It is somewhat slower than sending smoke signals.

Until a few weeks ago I got only one message. It was from one of my daughters, who was curious to see if this would work.

Now I get text messages every day. They are all from strangers. Some of them want to refinance my mortgage (I don't have one) or sell me prescription drugs I don't need. Quite a few are from young women. Many seem to be named Megan, and although I don't fully understand what they are offering I don't believe it will have broad appeal among elderly clergy.

My phone announces the arrival of text messages with a pretty little tune of my choosing. It plays that tune a lot now. I may have to change to something less intrusive, like a bugle call or a fire siren.

Soon after anything new has been invented someone discovers a way to make it annoying. Telephones have become more versatile. When they did it was certain that Spam would move from the Internet to the telephone. Spam is a kind of digital mad cow disease.

Inventors and entrepreneurs create a new and better world. They are followed by people who neither invent nor develop. They are the anti-entrepreneurs, who joylessly take the pleasure out of the inventions of others.

Civil libertarians will assert that these Spam merchants have a right to free speech. I agree, if they will do their speaking in their own home, at their own expense, and without invading my space and using my time. If they will follow those rules I will not even notice them. I don't want to censor what they say. I just want them to say it to someone else.

# Galley Slaves in Century Twenty One

The tunnel that connects England with France is a marvel of engineering, but it will never be a tourist attraction. Unlike the Empire State Building, the Roman Coliseum, or the Panama Canal, there is nothing to see. You can create the same experience without leaving home. Go into a closet, close the door, and sit in the dark for twenty minutes.

It is, however, a superior way to get from London to Paris. Its sleek Eurostar trains leave and arrive in the center of each city, unlike airlines which start and end in the distant hinterlands. Weather can cause a trip to be delayed or cancelled, but it takes a flood, blizzard or other major catastrophe to do it. It is much less likely to have problems than the tightly scheduled airlines, where a fog in Kansas City can throw the entire system into confusion.

Best of all, there is plenty of room on the train. Grown men and women can sit in comfort in train seats. Airlines are eager to avoid bankruptcy by packaging their customers as tightly as possible. They have gone about as far as they can go with this. The only people comfortable on a plane are those who are either traveling on expense accounts or able to upgrade to business class with frequent flyer miles. If coach passengers had oars to lean on they would be as comfortable as galley slaves.

Every kind of travel involves some degree of discomfort. Not even Eurostar offers a seat as comfortable as the one in my living room. Restaurants in Europe offer elegant food, but I always come home longing for baked beans, a hamburger, and a really cold glass of milk. Did you ever try to get a cold glass of milk in a restaurant that has a French menu?

I'm sure that visitors from other countries who come to the United States miss the comforts they enjoyed at home.

# God Does Things Differently

Hurricane Charley blew through Sanibel Island this summer. I have affectionate memories of winter visits to Sanibel. We went there for the first time when Sanibel was a barely inhabited sand spur, reached by a little ferry that chugged lazily across San Carlos Bay

There were few places to stay on the island then, and only a general store for basic supplies. We spent a lot of time swatting mosquitoes. The only other entertainment was the Volunteer Fire Department Fourth of July Fish Fry.

Our children were small when we first visited Sanibel. Now my grandchildren are nearly grown, and their memories will be of a different Sanibel. The mosquitoes have gone. Shops and restaurants and bars have defeated the retreating jungle. The sand roads have been paved and clogged with day trippers. On the whole, I liked the mosquitoes and the firemen better.

Sanibel changed slowly over the decades. It changed again suddenly in a few hours on August 13. One was the act of city planners. The other we call an act of God.

Sanibel has been over-run by surging storm waters before, and it will be again. It is a barrier island, a forward outpost against the encroaching waters, and it is the nature of barrier islands to be vulnerable.

Change is inevitable, whether it comes at the hands of developers and zoning specialists or in the blast of a hurricane. We can no more escape the one than the other. There are some changes that we plan, and some that fall upon us suddenly. Either way, the consequences are seldom what we expect.

The right question about every change is never why it happened. It is what we shall do now that it has happened. The past is settled. The future is up to us.

We are not likely to know whether any change is good or bad for a very long time. That is a question for historians, not politicians. What ultimately matters is not how good we are at planning. It is how well we adapt to what happens, whether we planned it or not.

God's ways are not our ways. We should be thankful they aren't.

# Noble to Forgive, Dishonest to Forget

In the 1920's the Ku Klux Klan in Indiana was powerful. It controlled legislatures and threatened politicians at every level. All that ended abruptly when the Chief Klucker, a man named D.C. Stevenson, was found in a Pullman car with the body of a young woman he had strangled.

Stevenson was sentenced to life in prison. After he went to prison his followers discovered the Christian virtue of forgiveness. Every year they petitioned the governor for Stevenson's release. He had repented, they said, and it is noble to forgive and forget.

Every year the governor is said to have responded with the same question: "The girl is still dead, isn't she?"

She was, of course, and her parents and siblings still lived and grieved. The politicians who were corrupted by the Klan still fouled the state. Forgiving Stevenson would not change history so that the evil he did never happened. It did happen, and forgiving Stevenson couldn't change that. His acts could be forgiven, but their consequences still haunted us.

We all need a lot of forgiveness, and faith is the belief that we are indeed forgiven. Forgiveness, however, is not a way for us to escape responsibility. It makes us more responsible, not less. Forgiveness does not rewrite our personal history, leaving out the unpleasant parts. It makes us strong enough to take up the burden of our past and carry it bravely but with sorrow.

We have all said words we wish we could call back. We can be forgiven for them, but that doesn't unsay what we said. We have done things we regret. We can be forgiven for them, but that doesn't undo what was done. The wounds we inflicted still bleed, the hurt we caused still aches.

Forgiveness sets us free from our past. It doesn't erase it. It liberates us from repeating regrettable acts. It gives us control over who we are and who we will become. It doesn't change what we once were.

Forgiveness overcomes evil by healing it, not denying it. It is noble to forgive. It is dishonest to forget. If the wrong were never done, we would not need to be forgiven.

# This World Is Not Our Reward

When terrorists deliberately kill children or a hurricane destroys homes we ask the same question: What did these innocents do to deserve this?

In both cases the answer is that they didn't deserve it. The rain falls and the wind blows on the just and the unjust. Terrorists choose victims because they are vulnerable, not because they deserve it. The weak and powerless are their preferred targets.

In a perfect world, only bad people would get sick, suffer from accidents, and lose what they value most. Good people would pass unscathed through terror and afflictions.

This is not a perfect world, or at least not perfect in that way. That is not what the world is designed to be. It is designed to be the theater for the war between good and evil, a war that is waged in every heart, including our own.

This is not Eden. When we left Eden, we left perfect justice and freedom from undeserved suffering behind. We can be just, but we can't always get justice. We can overcome suffering, but we can't always escape from it. There will be just as much justice in the world as we bring into it. The way past suffering is through it, not around it.

This world is not the reward for our heroism. It is the place where heroes are created. Evil will flourish for a time here. Temptations will abound. Our life will be disturbed by difficult choices. We will be confronted by sorrows we can neither avoid nor dismiss. We will be assaulted by people and events worse than our worst imaginings.

We will also see people behaving better than our best dreams. Firefighters will enter collapsing buildings; people will risk their lives for strangers. Our acquisitive society, obsessed with accumulating possessions, will face the destruction of possessions without complaint. When the worst happens, the best happens too.

That is what the world was designed to be. In that sense, it is a perfect world. In a world without evil events or evil people, nothing much would be required of us. In the real world much is required of us, and we can be equal to the challenge.

# Every Election is Judgment Day

To be born and live in a free society is a precious gift. Most people in most times have never known what it is to be free. It is difficult for people who are tyrannized to become free. It is also hard for those who have freedom to keep it. Freedom is a fragile blessing.

One reason it is hard to stay free is that democracy is a messy business. People in a democratic society should never see how their sausages or their laws are made. Too close an examination of the way we choose our leaders is not very edifying either. It is no more logical than the selection of a Dalai Llama, and a lot more expensive.

In an election, like in a war, a great deal of money is spent without producing anything useful. Unlike a war, an election usually appeals to greed more than sacrifice and to hatred rather than unity. People seldom come out of an election as better persons.

Although great, far-reaching issues are at stake most of the controversy is about things that don't matter at all. The goal of an election is to win power, not to establish truth. Promises are made and words are spoken with no other purpose than winning. A politician who loses is not a politician at all.

Democratic elections do not guarantee that freedom will be preserved. There are two paths to dictatorship. Some have seized power by arms, others by populism. They have won one election, and never permitted another. Either way works.

Every election is a judgment day. It judges not the candidates but the voters. In an election we demonstrate the values that drive us. We vote hopefully or hatefully, nobly or basely. We show who we are and what we want.

Despite this our democracy has lasted for a very long time. That can only be because it is a gift from God. If it were only a human achievement our freedom would never have survived the flawed people we are.

The wonderful thing about democratic elections is not that we get the best possible leaders. It is that we get the leaders we deserve.

# Relying On the Kindness of Strangers

We all sometimes depend upon the kindness of strangers. When we do we should ask who these strangers are, and why they are kind.

We were in Florida between hurricanes. We came in a hurry and were making our plans as we went along. I had phoned every hotel chain within forty miles of Vero Beach. At every attempt I got the same reply. All were solidly booked for three weeks with the repair crews that had come from distant states.

We went into one of the few restaurants that were operating, one of a chain. A well dressed man, apparently from out of town, was directing the staff. Out of all the people coming into the restaurant he spoke to me.

"Are you looking for a place to stay?"

When I said I was, he told me that the night before he had gone over to the beach. A few small resorts there had rooms. He gave me three phone numbers. At the second try I found the rooms we needed.

I knew who he was. He was an angel. Why else would he ask this question? Why else did he ask it of me?

Most people think that angels are creatures with wings that spend a lot of time playing the harp and looking wistful. Actually, the Greek word that is translated as "angel" means "someone sent with a message, a messenger". That isn't just its Biblical meaning. It has meant that since the time of Homer.

My angel was probably a district manager for the restaurant chain, pitching in to help in an emergency. That was his day job, and he was sent there by the company. But he was also moved to help strangers in trouble. For that he was sent by someone else.

After I left he would go back to his waiters and dishwashers, and continue his culinary duties. He was only a part-time angel. Most of the angels we meet are part-time.

He was a part-time angel, and he was kind because he was sent to be kind. That leads to the third question.

Have I ever been sent on such a mission? Did I go?

# I Never Lend Books

I buy a lot of books. Most ministers do. It must have something to do with seminary training. After you've read Xenophon's Anabasis in the original Greek any book looks better.

The dean of the seminary I attended had a great personal library. The walls of one room were lined with bookcases from floor to ceiling. All the books were murder mysteries. He was a great scholar and a gentle, kindly man. I suspect that room was where he escaped from an overdose of scholarship, gentleness and kindness in his life.

There are two reasons to buy a book. One is to learn something you didn't know. The other is to avoid learning anything at all. Both are good reasons.

I never lend books, but if I enjoy a book I often give it to someone. I don't care what they do with the book, with one exception. They can't bring it back to me. If I wanted it I wouldn't have given it to them. If they return it I have to find someone else to give it to.

People sometimes want to lend a book to me. That is meant kindly, but I would rather they didn't. If I borrow a book I have to read it promptly and return it. I have accumulated a lot of guilt from borrowed books. I forgot to return them or misplaced them or maybe absent-mindedly gave them to someone else. I have enough things to feel guilty about without that.

People who read books are never bored or lonely. There are whole worlds waiting for them to explore. On the other hand, they feel lost when they have nothing to read. I have sometimes been reduced to reading cereal boxes when there was nothing else at hand. There is a lot to read on a cereal box.

There are exceptions, but most religions have a book. The books are very different from one another. The purpose of a religion's book is to tell who the people are, and why they are, and what they should be. If the book tells the truth about that, it is not just a book. It is The Book.

# Keeping Up With the Neighbors

The Ten Commandments have a long list of things we are forbidden to covet. It lists your neighbor's wife, slaves, cattle, donkey and "anything else your neighbor owns." Modern neighbors are unlikely to have slaves, cattle or donkeys. There is still a little wife coveting going on, but we know it leads to tears.

The real coveting today is in that "anything else." To bring the commandment up to date we should include "You shall not covet your neighbor's technology." Technology envy is our generation's temptation.

There is a lot to covet. Every year brings a new set of automobile accessories that we can covet. Hardly anybody wants to crank windows up and down now, although it is not all that hard to do. Instead we want a car that tells us many things we don't need to know and a few we do. We want blue headlights and a variety of things that beep. We want buttons that do things we never wanted to do before. Nobody famous noticed it but a car without gadgets is like a day without sunshine.

The trouble with envying your neighbor's technology is that technology is a moving target. New gadgets come and go quickly. Hardly anybody remembers 8-track tapes or Betamax, but once they were briefly coveted. Nobody covets VHS now. DVD has pushed it aside, and it won't last long. Anything digital inspires a little lust right now. I've had my PDA for a little over a year. It won't connect to the Internet though, so I'm already coveting one that does.

Some things are eternal, but that doesn't mean they are good. Greed, pride, and the desire to make others envy us are as common as ever. Stealing an identity is harder than stealing a cow, but it is the same kind of sin. High technology theft is still theft, it is just faster. The new man is just the old Adam, suitably trendy. The more we change, the more we are the same.

The objects we desire change, but the way we desire them doesn't. Coveting a donkey and coveting a digital camera are much the same. Neither one brings any lasting happiness.

# Invisible, But Not Unreal

I made some new friends last week without seeing them. I was undergoing a procedure at a local clinic. In medical talk a procedure is something that is less than an operation but more than you wish it were.

This particular procedure was performed in a room with several gurneys separated by curtains. The doctor went about inflicting painful acts on a number of patients. When I was assaulted there were two other persons in the room. I couldn't see them but I could hear every word and groan. A young mother was in the cubicle next to me. Across the room was a man who, like the doctor, was from Texas.

The doctor talked to each of us all the time when he was with us, either to distract us from what he was doing or because he was a naturally sociable being. He asked each their age, talked about their families and their work, and even told an occasional joke.

(Texas insider joke:

Question: What does a University of Texas grad call a Texas A&M grad five years after they graduate?

Answer: Boss.)

I felt I knew these people well, even though I couldn't see them. I knew about their children, and I knew the sounds they made when they were in pain. I knew that the man was from out of town, and that the woman's mother had recently died. They knew that I was a minister, which left the doctor uncertain about what sort of joke was appropriate.

The young woman was about to give up a professional career and take a new job. Her mother's sickness and death had changed her priorities in a remarkable way. She was going to work in the hospital, on the 11 pm to 7 am shift in the emergency room.

Before accepting the job she had observed the ER. She knew that in the night the patients were mostly intoxicated, people with serious pain, or the victims of automobile accidents. She was not deterred. She came to help, not because of what they were, but because of what she was.

I didn't see these people, but I know that they exist. I haven't seen God either. Like my invisible clinic friends, I know God by what God does.

# A Frenzied Squirrel

When I leave the parking garage at a local hospital the person who collects the toll always has a smile and a friendly word. At least, almost always.

Last week as I held out the ticket the man went berserk. He shrieked and appeared to be trying to climb up the wall of his little booth, slapping his leg frantically. He has never done this before. I wondered what I could have done to provoke him.

"He climbed right up my pants leg!" he cried. Then a squirrel leaped out of the door of his booth and scrambled across the pavement. It was an upsetting experience for all of us: for the parking attendant, for me, and for the squirrel.

At the critical moment none of us understood what was happening. The toll collector only knew that he was being attacked by something furry and extremely active. I only knew that this normally unexceptional man had suddenly turned into a raving maniac. All the squirrel knew was – well, who knows what the squirrel knew. He certainly wasn't having a good day.

It is safe to say that for a moment all three of us were terrified, and none of us needed to be. None of us, not even the squirrel, was in any real danger. All the adrenalin we were pumping was quite unnecessary.

I once visited a leper colony, in the days before the disease was treatable and its name was changed to Hansen's disease. Leprosy is not always painful. It causes its victims to be unable to feel pain in arms and legs, fingers and toes. This is not a blessing, but a curse. Without pain a leper could suffer terrible burns without knowing it, have wounds that bled unnoticed.

Fear is like pain. The only thing worse than being afraid or feeling pain, is being unable to feel fear or pain. A fearless person will have an exciting but short life.

None of us likes to feel fear or pain. We wonder why God permits them. They are not however a mistake in the way we were created. We are designed to survive, and fear and pain help us survive.

# Faith Is Not a Commodity

Have you ever ridden with a bus driver who was an Elvis impersonator?

This year I've made a lot of trips through the Orlando airport. I rent cars from a company that isn't in the terminal. They use shuttle buses to take you back and forth. On one trip I was the only passenger.

"This is just my day job," the driver told me. "I'm really in the entertainment business. I play trumpet, and I'm an impersonator. I sing all of the Elvis songs."

He didn't look like the King at all, but maybe he does a better job with costume and make-up.

"I even wrote a song for Elvis, but he never sang it. It's called Our Love Is Like the Snow (It seems to come and go.)"

It didn't take much encouragement for him to sing. The trip was long enough for two stanzas and a chorus.

The song came from the drivers' childhood in Elkhart, Indiana, where there is a lot of snow. Elvis grew up in Tennessee. Maybe that's why he didn't appreciate the lyrics.

You don't often get a shuttle bus with professional entertainment. You seldom notice the person who drives the bus. This one was an interesting person. He had a story to tell.

Everybody has a story to tell. There are no uninteresting people. There are just people whose story we don't know yet.

People, like snow flakes, are created one at a time, each of us unique. We each come with a different mix from the limitless variations of the gene pool. We each have experiences that are shared by no other. Sometimes it is said of a remarkable person that "they broke the mold after he was made." That's true of all of us.

That's why faith is such an intensely personal experience. Faith is the encounter between the Creator and the created. God is the same, yesterday and today and forever. Each of us is different from every other. Every encounter with God is unlike all the rest, not because God changes but because we are each unique.

We can tell people about our faith, but what they experience will always be their own.

# A Different Kind of Thanksgiving

One year when I was asked to give a Thanksgiving talk I tried not to repeat the bromides that Thanksgiving speakers traditionally serve up. I titled my talk "Thanksgiving from the Point of View of the Turkey." Although it left the audience a little puzzled, it certainly gave them a fresh perspective.

For bad judgment it ranked along with my famous Mothers' Day sermon, which I based on certain Biblical mothers. Unwisely I chose as one example Herodias, who told her daughter to ask for the head of John the Baptist. I also mentioned Jezebel, and we all know what she was. There are mothers now gray who still remember that Sunday, and not with pleasure.

My only excuse was that I was very young and still believed that anything different was bound to be good. That isn't always true. The advertising slogan "new and improved" must be taken with a dose of skepticism. Sometimes it means "We changed the package and cheapened the product."

Of course, sometimes the new model actually is improved. It depends on the reason for the changes. If it was changed to make the product better it probably will. If it was changed only to make it different that's all it will succeed in doing.

In the 1970's there was a lot of talk of "the new morality." This turned out to be mainly about sex and drugs. The new morality was remarkably like the old dissipation. It wasn't new, and it wasn't moral. It was only different.

A favorite theme of populist dictators is that they will bring "a new world order." The operative word is "order". They will force obedience to their plan, which is the same as every other tyrant's plan. The plan is that the Leader will take everything and give you what he thinks you should have. Karl Marx just invented a new terminology for what Alexander the Great did without trying to justify it.

In the long scheme of things there is progress. But it is not progress in a line straight line forward. We have to sort through a lot of bad ideas to find a few good ones.

# We Don't Live In Heaven Yet

It can't be December yet. I'm still trying to finish October. Now Thanksgiving is over and we've started down the toboggan slide toward Christmas. There are cards to address, gifts to buy and wrap, trips to plan, and it all has to be done right away. The calendar with its flying pages is our enemy.

The Friday after Thanksgiving is called "Black Friday" by retailers and their accountants. It is the day when they hope crowds of shoppers will let them use black ink in their ledgers after months of alarming red. Economists look anxiously at the sales statistics. For once the fate of the nation is not in the hands of the Federal Reserve or the Congress or the military. It is the lowly shopper, harried and weary, who holds the reins. If the shopper falters, Wall Street panics.

It seems strange that the health of the nation depends not just on what we produce but on what we consume. But it doesn't matter how much we produce if nobody wants the product. That is the hard lesson that was taught by the collapse of Marxist economies. Factories that turned out great quantities of shoddy goods were a failure. It is the shopper who enforces quality. What the shopper rejects won't be produced for very long in a free society.

Every holiday season there are voices that denounce the commercialization of Christmas or Hanukah or whatever holiday we celebrate at the end of the year. They are almost right. The still small voice of faith can be drowned out by the jingle of cash registers and the clamor of advertising. The Psalmist who heard God say, "Be still, and know that I am God" spoke truly. Faith is the ability to hear whispers, not shouts.

But we practice our faith in the busy world, not in heaven. This is where we live and breathe, work and pray. This is where the hungry wait for food and the oppressed dream of freedom. We don't have the luxury of celebrating our faith in the calm of a monastery. We are called to be faithful in spite of the noise and confusion around us.

# Mr. Sears and Mr. Roebuck

Mr. Sears and Mr. Roebuck saw that there were lots of farm families that didn't get to town very often, so they sent their store to them. Or more accurately, they sent a catalog and let people order what they needed by mail. In the 19th century this was a great convenience.

Most people can get to a store now, but they can't always find a place to park. If they get parked, they can't always find a clerk to help them. If they find a clerk, they discover that there only a few things to choose from.

Henry Ford said that customers for his Model T could have any color they wanted, as long as it was black. Stores offer more choices than that, but there are limits. No store can carry every possible choice. The color we want or the size we need may be the one they don't have.

The modern equivalent to mail order shopping is shopping online. Instead of being frustrated shopping at a mall, we may choose to be frustrated peering at a computer at home.

The Internet vastly expands our choices. Sometime it expands them too much. When a search engine responds to our question with 350,000 possibilities we are worse off than if it only gave us one. Too many choices are as troubling as too few. Today we have an overwhelming number of choices. Do we need so many decisions?

Instead of Ford's black we can choose from an infinite number of colors, some of which were invented by an ad agency. You can buy a car of a color described as "cashmere". What kind of color is that? Cashmere sweaters come in a dozen colors. Are they trying to tell me that their car is warm and fuzzy?

We used to refresh our self when shopping by having a cup of coffee. You can't do that any more. There are sixteen kinds of coffee, all of them three times as expensive as a plain cup of java. Nothing is simple any more.

One thing hasn't changed. No many how many choices we have, some choices are right and some are wrong.

# We All Know Scrooge

Dickens' Christmas Carol comes back every winter like an old friend who comes home for the holidays. Every male actor who treads the boards has a try at playing Scrooge. Even the animated Mr. Magoo took a shot at it.

Scrooge is the only decent role in the story. The ghosts don't offer much scope, Bob Cratchett and his family don't have any good lines, and even Tiny Tim has a supporting role only slightly more prominent than the Christmas goose. It's the miserly Scrooge who invites exaggeration, bringing out the ham in otherwise normal actors.

If Scrooge is a villain he is a believable one. He doesn't take pleasure in the suffering of others, or inflict pain for the sake of pain. He has power over the people who work for him, but he doesn't seek power. He just accepts it, uses it for his own needs, and ignores everyone else. He certainly would not think of himself as a bad person.

Scrooge encounters reality in his nightshirt, not in his working clothes. He has all these bad dreams, but his dreams are truer than what he sees when he is awake. At first he interprets his dreams in the light of what he knows about the real world. He thinks they are the result of eating too many carbohydrates. In the end he realizes that though his intellect can't make sense of his dreams, his dreams make sense of his life.

We like this old tale because nearly everybody can think of someone like Scrooge. We are just lucky if we don't work for them. A fortunate few see a little deeper, and see the Scrooge in their own life. We have all done harm not because we are evil, but merely because we are practical. We let what we know about the world dictate what we believe about it.

In the end Scrooge sees that he lives in two worlds. One he can see with his eyes and record as profit and loss in his ledgers. The other world is as invisible as love or integrity. He can make his home in whichever world he chooses. So can we.

# Never Throw Away the Instructions

Like everything else, Christmas has been altered by technology. The change is not for the better. Once you could understand your gifts. They were things like neckties or cologne. You knew what they were and what to do with them.

Increasingly these useful gifts are being replaced by electronics that are a frustration to the technologically challenged. It began decades ago with the video tape recorder. Many of them blinked "12:00" endlessly because nobody over the age of sixteen knew how to program them. They aren't a problem now. They have become obsolete.

Instead we have devices we have never seen before. (If you have seen them they are already obsolete.) There are telephones that recognize their owner's voice when properly trained, cameras that take pictures without film when properly installed, and machines that record television programs and play them back later when they are properly prompted. The sinister word is "properly."

Technology is unforgiving. One improper action will cause unexpected events or no event at all. As a public service I am offering some advice to those wondering what on earth to do with their Christmas gifts.

First, never throw away the instruction book. It may appear to be written by a drunk who knows English only as a second language. It may include chapters telling you how to do things you have no intention of ever doing. Keep it. It is the only tenuous contact you have with the demons who designed this thing.

As a backup to the instruction book many devices include a phone number for what is laughingly called "technical support." Before dialing this number be sure that you are prepared. Have something nearby that you can read while you listen to recorded music and the repeated claim that your call is important to them.

Technology gives new meaning to the phrase "a little child shall lead them." Small children who can't make change can operate these things in ways that humiliate their elders. This is good for our souls. It forces us to admit that we aren't perfect.

That's a good beginning. The next step is admitting that we are imperfect in other ways, and need someone who can forgive us.

# After the Terror Is Over

The world has learned a new word. It is a synonym for destruction, suffering and death. The word is tsunami.

The earth moved, the waters rose, and unimaginable chaos struck. The worst nightmares Hollywood can construct were exceeded. Families were shattered. Survivors searched for lost kin. Thousands are both homeless and bereaved.

Death, bereavement, and loss are writ large in such a disaster. But the loss of one person is always severe to those who suffer it. When someone you love suffers or dies it makes no great difference whether it is a solitary loss or a hundred thousand others suffer at the same time. The mass disaster only makes many ask the same questions we all ask one at a time.

They are terrible questions, questions we usually avoid. A great disaster or our own solitary loss forces us to think about them.

We ask where God is in all this. Why do such things happen? Does God cause it, or permit it? Does God save one and abandon another? Is it part of some great Godly plan that sacrifices people for a cause we don't understand?

These are terrible questions but not the first ones we must ask. There are more basic questions that could render these questions moot.

Who are we that this should happen to us?

We are, all of us, creatures that die. This is the one undeniable fact that we all want to deny. When we are young we know we will die, but not for a very long time. It is such a long time that we can put the idea aside for now. But whether we think about it or not, we know that all our lives will end the same way. We will die.

The important question is not why we die, whether singly or in thousands. The question is about what dying means. Is it the end of everything or the beginning of more? Are we simply creatures that die or candidates for eternity? What has happened to those who died?

To understand what life means we must know what dying means. That is something that only faith can understand.

# We All Want To Be Loved

Pundits are professionals whose job it is to have an opinion about everything. Lately some pundits have been speculating that the Arab street will think more kindly of us because of our tsunami relief efforts. Maybe our charity will be cost effective.

It would be better if they turned their massive intellects to a more useful question, like who will win the Super Bowl. If charity is profitable, it isn't charity. It is a business transaction. It is not about caring and giving. It is about buying.

Asking this question is an insult to the people who were moved to contribute. It implies that they are not generous but calculating. It is an insult to the people who are helped. It assumes that their friendship can be bought. Neither is true.

Individuals all over the world gave because their hearts were moved by sympathy, not because they thought they would gain by it. Governments poured out money because their citizens expected no less.

Americans have a pathetic longing to be loved by other people. Terrorists do not frighten us so much as puzzle us. We cannot understand why they hate us so much. We long to make them like us.

That is the worst possible reason to relieve the suffering of distant people. It is bad because it won't work. If we give because we hope for gratitude, we will be disappointed.

It is not just more blessed to give than to receive. It is also more enjoyable. Those who give feel good about it. Those who receive feel inferior. People who are rich and generous should not count on the gratitude of those who are poor and desperate. It requires an even more noble spirit to be grateful than to be generous. That is why it is said that no good deed goes unpunished.

We do not need to be repaid for helping suffering people, not even with gratitude. That is not the reason people all over the world gave so much.

Terrorists hate us because of who they are, not who we are. We won't change that with charitable gifts. We help because we care. They kill because they hate.

# The Difference Between Theology and Faith

I have a friend who is a poet. That's not his day job, but he does it well. He can paint a picture of the prairies that makes you see what he sees. He doesn't just tell about scenery, though. Often he paints himself into the picture, telling what he feels or where his mind wanders. Snow on the street is one thing, but someone walking in that snow is a richer picture. People are more interesting than scenery.

My friend tells about his surroundings, but he tells more about himself. Everyone has a story, and all the stories are fascinating.

Like music, poetry communicates what plain language can't contain. Poetry would be useless for an instruction manual for a cell phone. Poems explore realms that manual writers would not dare to enter.

Truth has a different meaning for the poet than for the manual writer. It doesn't mean counting the nuts and bolts correctly. For the poet truth means accurately communicating an elusive reality. It means letting us know the person who walks in the snow, not describing the snowflakes.

The language of poets and musicians is different from the language of engineers and scientists. The poet's truth is about things that can't be measured or counted. It is about love and hatred, about beauty and ugliness. It is about what we are, not what we pretend. It is about what we do, and why we do it.

We owe a tremendous debt to engineers and scientists. They have lengthened our life span and lifted us out of the brutish misery of a rich society. But there is more to life than living well for a long time. In poverty and prosperity we ask the same questions, feel the same needs. They are the questions and needs of living people.

That is the difference between theology and faith. Theology is something we talk about. Faith is something we experience. A lecture about theology is mildly interesting to people who are not theologians. It becomes important when the speaker puts himself into the scene, like the person walking in the snow.

People are more interesting than scenery.

# The High Cost of Stupidity and Immorality

I have a new cell phone. Cell phone companies will give you a free or discounted phone if you sign a contract for two years. Since the phones last for about two years this keeps you on their plantation. All those television commercials are wasted on those of us who are in cell phone bondage.

It does keep me up to date on technology. Every two years I get a phone that is smaller and more complicated than the last.

This phone does a lot of things that I have no intention of learning to do. All I ask of a phone is that it have a reasonable battery life and doesn't embarrass me in public places. Most phones meet this standard if I remember to turn them off in church, movie theaters, and concert halls. That part is up to me.

I'll confess that sometimes I talk while I'm driving. If a phone rings it is hard not to answer it. Besides, we are all pressed for time. Talking and driving is a form of multi-tasking, and multi-tasking is in vogue right now. A good driver should be able to do it. Hardly anybody doubts that they are a good driver.

Whether cell phones are a blessing or a curse depends on who uses them. It is possible to talk on a phone while driving in heavy traffic, but nobody makes you do it. Don't blame Motorola or Nokia for all the people engaged in earnest conversation on the freeways. Technology doesn't make people dumber. It just raaises the cost of stupidity.

We are surrounded by devices that make life easier and more rewarding. Our pioneer ancestors would be amazed by all the things we can do with electronics. Our powers have been vastly expanded.

Expanded powers mean greater responsibility. We can take pretty good pictures without knowing much about photography. But the camera won't decide what pictures we take. The same digital camera that takes flawless family mementoes can be used for pornography. We choose which we will use it to do.

Morality doesn't change in the age of electronics. It just becomes more expensive.

# Remember the Martyrs

Everybody loves a bargain. That's why there are discount stores and discount airlines. Cruise lines offer two-for-one sales, cutting in half a fare that no one has ever actually paid. We relish the thought that we are saving money.

A low price isn't always a bargain. Sometimes it's just cheap, which is quite different. It isn't quite true that you always get what you pay for, but you seldom get more than you pay for. Shabby merchandise is no bargain, no matter how low the price.

It is possible to get a college degree without learning very much. A judicial choice of easy courses and an effort just sufficient to get by will do the trick. It can be four or five enjoyable years, education on the cheap. In the long run it is worth as little as it cost.

Marriage can be the biggest commitment of a lifetime or a casual arrangement. It can be merely a temporary co-habitation, with one or both partners investing little of themselves. A marriage at the lowest cost will miss completely the union of two souls that marriage can be.

A job can be a calling, work we are suited to do and want to do as well as we can. It doesn't have to be all that. We can do it just well enough to get by, a bargain career.

We all love our country. For some that is a costly affection. It can lead to high risks and deadly peril. Patriotism need not be so costly. We can want the rewards of freedom without risking anything for it.

Faith can be a pleasant enjoyment of positive thoughts. We can praise God for the unlikely love given to us, confident of continued blessings. We can fashion a religion that never changes us, never demands anything of us, and never contemplates unpleasant realities.

Dietrich Bonhoeffer, a German theologian, wrote about "cheap grace", the desire for bargain-price religion. Grace did not come cheaply for him. He was safe in America, but he returned to Germany to keep the faith alive under Nazi rule. They hanged him.

If you pray for God's will to be done, don't forget about the martyrs.

# The Day After the End of the World

Maybe you're not worried about suicidal terrorists, tidal waves, mud slides or serial killers. There is something else you can worry about: chickens. Chickens could kill millions of people, destroy every economy in the world, and end civilization as we know it.

Or maybe they won't.

Disease control specialists live in dread of a virus that has been spread in Asia by birds. Wild birds carry the virus but aren't harmed by it. They give it to chickens which are killed by the virus, but may be the bridge to infecting mammals like us. If it is spread by humans the effect would be devastating. No country in the world is safe. No country is prepared for such an outbreak.

A hundred years ago nobody needed to worry about deadly diseases on the other side of the world. They stayed on the other side of the world. Today we are blessed with communication that has drawn the world together. China is just a jet flight away, and a lot of jets are flying.

The same technology that brings tee shirts across the Pacific can bring things that are neither planned nor welcome. Technology is both our blessing and our curse. When the world becomes a village, the whole village can get sick.

Nobody knows when or even if this will happen. What is known is that it could, and that if it does it will be devastating. It will be a doomsday pandemic. We will all be victims, not of a nuclear holocaust, but of a humble virus.

There has always been speculation about the end of the world. Ignoring the Biblical injunction that nobody can know when the world will end, some have been bold enough to predict the date. Until now they have all been wrong.

We don't need to know when the world will end. We can be sure that for us it will end in a measurable number of years. We will all die, if not all together, then surely one by one.

The real question is not when the world will end. It is what will come after the world ends, whether for you and me or for everyone.

# Moderation Isn't Everything

There are two conflicting trends in restaurants today. The newer one is less food. Sometimes it's called a "small plate," or the Portuguese word "tapas" is used. Instead of a rack of lamb there is a lamb chop or two, or a single fish filet is served. If you want more food, you order more than one plate.

The older trend is the all-you-can eat buffet. The food may be good, and there is certainly lots of it. This is a bargain for lumberjacks, iron workers, and the offensive line of a football team. More sedentary types pay for the excesses of others.

A bar that advertised "all you can drink" would be a social crime. Too much food is not as dangerous as too much alcohol, but it isn't anything to celebrate either. The only people who should eat all they can are those who, like polar bears, are preparing to hibernate for the winter. In a nation where obesity has become pandemic "all you can eat" is not the same as "all you should eat."

There are two kinds of eating problems: too little food, or too much. The distended bellies of starving children are one disturbing extreme. The distended bellies of fat buffet warriors represent another. Those who voluntarily starve are anorexic. Those who voluntarily overeat are obese.

It is tempting to believe in the adage of moderation in all things. Eat moderately, drink moderately and live long. But life isn't that simple. Moderation is good in some things, but not in all things.

To be moderately faithful in marriage isn't good enough. To love your children moderately will leave them starved for affection. A moderately honest person is not someone you want to buy a used car from.

Good, gray moderate people aren't just boring. They easily become unwilling accomplices in evil. There was no moderate response to the Holocaust. If Martin Luther King had been moderately critical of injustice the world would be a different place today. Some things are worth dying for, which is a most immoderate response.

Moderation is good at the dinner table, but not everywhere. Some occasions demand a bigger commitment than that.

# Politics, Sports and Religion

Coaches and fans are both enthusiastic about sports. Both have strong opinions. The difference between a fan and a coach is that the coach can be fired if the team doesn't win. Nobody ever fires a fan.

Fans also have fewer rewards. There are no shoe contracts for fans.

Politics and sports are alike in some ways. Both raise powerful emotions. Both cause people to be certain they are right on very little evidence. In both every amateur feels qualified to criticize the professionals. In both winning is the most important thing. If you don't win, nothing else matters.

They are unlike in one way. In sports being wrong is costly for the coach but only a disappointment to the fans. In politics being wrong leads to suffering everyone shares.

Religion is like both sports and politics in some ways. Everybody has an opinion, and they often feel very strongly about it. That's why it's better not to discuss politics or religion or sports with strangers. You can usually disagree with friends, but a stranger may be prone to violence.

Democratic society doesn't depend on everyone having the same faith, the same political persuasion, and everybody being a Cubs fan. The road to democracy doesn't require converting everyone to being like us. It doesn't mean surrendering our deepest convictions in the interests of peace. Democracy requires people who can disagree about important things without rancor.

That isn't easy. It doesn't make it easier to pretend that there are no real differences between us. That may work for sports if we really like the game and not just a team. It won't work for more divisive commitments. We can't claim that all religions are really the same, because they aren't. We can't say politics doesn't matter, because it does.

Our country is deeply divided in politics, in religious convictions, and in the definition of morality. That isn't bad. What is bad is that our differences lead to bitterness, unscrupulous attacks, and the loss of common decency. Our hope is not that one side will finally overcome the other. It is that we will treat others the way we want them to treat us.

# Beyond Technology

I like gadgets. Not just computers and cell phones and digital cameras. Those were fun when they were new, but now they are so common they're boring. I have a personal air conditioner that hangs around my neck and blows cool air on my face. I own a device that not only serves as a date book and address list but remembers all my passwords, pin numbers, and prescriptions. It even contains two complete Bible translations.

Recently I bought a Snore Stopper. It's a little like those invisible electric fences that keep your dog from straying. You wear this device on your wrist like a watch. Two electrodes press against your skin. When the Snore Stopper detects snoring it gives a faint electrical shock, just enough to make the offender roll over. Supposedly it trains the offender to stop snoring. It may train me to stop sleeping.

We're still trying this out, but the concept is good. It appeals both to men who deny that they snore and to women who know the denial is a lie. A wife who considers her husband's latest combination telephone, camera, and birthday reminder excessive might approve of something that would muffle the noise at night.

I like all these things because I am the right age for them. I am young enough to accept them and old enough to say, "Gee whiz!" They don't appeal as much to people who have grown up with technology and think it is ordinary.

All my gadgets are part of our modern technology. Jacques Ellul, a French sociologist and theologian, believed that technology creates us more than we create it. Morality doesn't constrain technology. If it is possible to do something we will do it, whether it is moral or not.

Because it is possible to create nuclear weapons, clone mammals, or control minds those things will be done. Not everything technology enables is as harmless as a snort in the night.

I like my gadgets but I don't worship them. The only way to live in a dangerous world is to look beyond technology to define who we are and what we do. Technology doesn't distinguish between good and evil. God does.

# Playground of the Rich and Famous

Monte Carlo is a playground of the rich and famous. There are few cars recognizable to Americans parked in the Place de Casino. Instead there are the exotic products of Bentley, Ferrari, and Lamborghini. Millionaires are small fry on the French Riviera. It's the yachts of billionaires that compete for space in the tiny harbors.

It is to be expected that in such a rarified atmosphere the newest innovations should thrive. This year there is a novelty seen on every street corner in Monaco. There are cows, life-sized replicas of cows, each different from the next, each startling in its own way. There are polka dot cows and striped cows, cows in clothes of many kinds, even a cow with a nude figure reclining on its back.

It's a lot like Chicago in 1999. Chicago's whimsical summer has finally reached the Riviera.

Imitation is the most sincere form of flattery. It's comforting for an unsophisticated Midwesterner to find that his native state is ahead of the curve. The Beautiful People seldom come to Illinois, but they are welcome to copy our cows.

It's another example of the long reach of globalization. What is enjoyed in one country is soon prized in distant places. Americans are ordering cappuccinos while Nigerians drink Coca Cola. French songs are heard by Russian teen-agers on devices made in China.

The shrinking world has not however become more peaceful. It is an illusion to believe that if people know each other better they will love each other more. Anyone who has ever lived in a small town knows that familiarity does not always breed affection. The global village is just like the old fashioned kind: sometimes neighborly, sometimes filled with gossip, envy, and even hatred.

A peaceful world requires peaceable people, and we are a long way from being that. Better communication gives wings to evil ideas as well as saintly ones. The world is changing, but it will not be changed for the better until its people are. That is a change in our hearts, not our transportation.

Peace does not come from knowing people better. It comes from loving them more.

I hope they enjoy our cows in Monaco.

# Where Is the Absurd Eggplant?

When you travel in Europe you sometimes have to communicate with people who don't speak English. In a single week I have had to cope with Spanish, French, and Italian. I have found that speaking louder and slower does not help.

One answer is the phrase book. This is a small book that lists questions you might want to ask, and then supplies the translation. I have an electronic phrase book, which even pronounces the translated phrase on a tiny speaker. Since the native people seldom hear anyone talk through a tiny speaker, a foreigner imitating one can lead to confusion.

You may think you are asking where the rest room is, while the local person hears something quite different. Besides, if you get a reply you don't understand it.

American tourist: "Where is the absurd eggplant?"

Native speaker: "I think you are deranged."

American tourist: "Huh?"

This is why the first things you should learn are the phrases for "Please" and "Thank you." Then the conversation can go like this:

American tourist: "Where is the absurd eggplant please?"

Native speaker: "I think you are deranged."

American tourist: "Thank you."

The Old Testament says that God inflicted all these languages on us to keep us humble. It certainly works for me. It is impossible to believe I am one of the Lords of the Universe when I am rendered mute and powerless by cab drivers chattering with each other when I can't understand a word.

It may be that what the world needs now is love, sweet love; but humility runs a close second. There's not enough of that either. We are terribly concerned about building the self confidence of children. We construct contests where everyone is a winner. When a child strikes out in a ball game we cry "Good try!" We build self-esteem so strong that reality is left behind.

Sometimes we succeed too well. It may be true that you have to think like a winner to be a winner, but a winner who never loses is only half-wise. We learn from our defeats as well as our successes.

We are creatures, not the Creator. We need to remember that. A bientot!

# What Stays in Las Vegas

What happens in Las Vegas stays in Las Vegas, if you stay there with it. If you leave, you'll take it home with you.

Nobody meets you at the airport to give back the money you lost in Las Vegas. If it is no more than you can afford to lose you don't expect them to. Because you know you can lose, it is fun when you win.

You can lose things that aren't as tangible as money. Things like integrity or faithfulness or honesty. They aren't returned at the airport either.

The notion that you can have a time or place that is disconnected from the rest of your life is an adolescent fantasy. It is a dream of being free from normal restraint, free for acts that have no consequences. It is the fantasy that whispers "just this one time". That whisper is the beginning of many sorrows.

It is only a fantasy. Grown-ups should know better. What you do creates the person you are, and you can't escape from yourself.

There are a lot of good shows in Las Vegas, a variety of entertainment equaled in few other places. It is a change from the monotony of ordinary life. That's why it exists.

Las Vegas is neither better nor worse than anywhere else. Most people there are like most people anywhere. Those who are not would be the same wherever they were. A vacation trip is not a visit to another planet. It is part of the rest of your life.

Sometimes the fantasy ends unexpectedly. The consequence of our deeds catches up with us. We are overwhelmed by the discovery that we have become someone we don't want to be. For some that is the shattering of an illusion. For others it is the beginning of faith.

That can happen anywhere, not just at Las Vegas. We can't cut a piece out of our life. What we are is the result of what we have done, not of what life has done to us. We can't change what we have done. We can however be forgiven and we can forgive ourselves. That's enough hope for us to go on living.

# Propriety and the Elderly Female

I sometimes drive people who need a ride to a clinic or hospital. Referrals come from social agencies to a group that matches them with volunteers. It is a little help for the clients, very little trouble for the volunteers, and often enjoyable for both.

The passengers aren't a cross section of the community. They aren't all poor, but none of them belong to country clubs. They aren't all elderly, but they aren't teen-agers either. Some are heroic, having faced and overcome great challenges. All are interesting, in one way or another.

Not long ago I met a lady whose standards of morality (or perhaps propriety) exceed my own. She was a very senior citizen, considerably older than I am, and well advanced in what doctors call "the aging process." I drove her to a local clinic, waited while she underwent a procedure, and took her back to the senior apartments where she lives.

As we drove up to the door she thanked me and asked, "Can I give you something?"

I said the same thing I sometimes say to my mother-in-law: "You can give me a kiss on the cheek."

She looked at me with dark suspicion before she answered, "I think I'd rather give you money."

I was flattered. The last time I was suspected of having base designs on an acquaintance I was in junior high school. It was a surprise that time, too.

In some ways I was pleased with this encounter. I am glad she doesn't offer her affections freely. As recent events in New Orleans have pointed out, there is a great deal of evil in this world. Trusting people make evil possible, sometimes cooperating in their own victimization.

Distrust can become pathological, however. Trusting no one is even more dangerous than trusting everyone. It can make us flinch at shadows and turn aside from friendship. There is a risk in every relationship, but it is a risk we must take sometimes. The alternative is being forever alone.

Faith is a relationship with the Creator. It is risky, like all relationships. We might be wrong if we choose to trust God. We will certainly be lonely if we don't.

# Call Me Grandfather

When my first grandchild was born, I was asked what I wanted to be called. There are lots of names for grandparents that sound cute when a toddler lisps them: Popsi, Grampa, and Paw Paw come to mind. But I knew those children's names wouldn't be so cute if a 185 pound, six foot six college student said them. That day would surely come.

I said I wanted to be called "Grandfather, Sir."

That's partly because I have a particular image of a grandfather. He is a graying man who sits on a bench outside a cottage in the Alps. A little girl or boy sits at his feet, listening respectfully. The grandfather says something very, very wise. Then he gets up and goes in the cottage to make cuckoo clocks.

I got part of my wish. My grandsons call me "Grandfather", but they have never quite mastered the "Sir" part. Until now. At my 80th birthday celebration my 16 year old younger grandson called me "Grandfather, Sir."

"You've never said that before," I said. "But why did you say it now?"

"Because you've earned it."

I hadn't realized that "Sir" has to be earned. But sometimes it does. The accident of his birth made me his grandfather. It took a lot more than that to earn the "Sir." It took eighteen years of affection and trust.

We owe respect to every person, even those who aren't respectable. We must not take away the dignity of anyone. Every police officer is taught that. But neither must we cheapen honor by failing to give it where we choose. Respect is a matter of courtesy. Honor is a choice.

In our equalitarian society we can distribute honors so freely that no one is honored. When everyone gets a prize the prize no longer means anything.

It doesn't do any good to demand that people honor us. We don't have a right to be honored. We have to earn it. I'm not sure that I have, but I'm grateful for the possibility.

After my grandson called me "Grandfather, Sir" I said something very, very wise. Then I wondered if I could make a cuckoo clock.

# Cost Accounting

I almost got a nice birthday present, but ended up getting a nicer one.

I frequently drive a very nice lady from Rantoul to Urbana for dialysis treatments. (I'll call her Lois, since that isn't her name.) I think all of her drivers look forward to seeing Lois. She is invariably cheerful, interested in everyone around her, and always a lift to tired spirits.

Lois isn't a silent passenger. She becomes part of your life, and you of hers. That's why I wasn't surprised to learn that she planned to buy a birthday present for me. I would have prized it, but I didn't get it. I got something better.

"Sunday there was a missionary at my church who was collecting money to help a sister congregation in New Orleans," she told me. "I gave him all the extra money I had." That included the money she planned to use to buy a present for me.

She didn't know that she gave me a bigger gift than any she would have found in a store. She probably gave that missionary the largest gift he received that day. The size of a gift is determined not by its value in dollars and cents, but in what was given up to make it.

Like most people, I give money to a lot of different causes. Some of them are very small contributions, some big enough to help a little. None of them change the way I live. It is money I didn't need and didn't miss.

Famous foundations honor the names of captains of industry who accumulated huge sums. I doubt if any of their endowments substantially changed the lives of the donors or of their heirs. It was money that, like my little charities, was not really missed.

That's the point of the Biblical story of the widow's mite, a tiny contribution that cost more than the casual gift of the wealthy. It is also behind the statement that there is no greater love than this, that one person lay down their life for another.

Some people do lay down their life for another, but they do it one day at a time.

# Self Esteem and the Dalai Lama

The Dalai Lama didn't have a normal childhood, even for a Tibetan. Instead of going to kindergarten he was home schooled in Buddhist theology. He was told from childhood that he was the reincarnation of his country's ancient spiritual leader. That's not quite the same as being told that you are God, but it is close. It is certainly a defense against low self esteem.

While still a teen-ager the Dalai Lama was exiled to India, along with a few thousand of his followers. The Communist conquerors of Tibet had plans for Tibet that didn't include a reincarnated Lama.

Since then this young man has become a world traveler, visiting every country that welcomes him. He has hobnobbed with presidents and popes. He is a celebrity in his own right.

As the spiritual leader of his people he made an unusual contribution to their religious life. He changed the curriculum of Tibetan monastic schools. To the debates over ancient Buddhist writings he has added Physics 101.

This is in keeping with his belief that science and spirituality are both necessary to understanding the world. He believes that either by itself gives only half the picture, and knowing half the truth is worse than knowing none at all. Buddhist monks need to know about quantum mechanics, and presumably physicists could benefit from being schooled in spirituality.

This sounds good, but there are some problems with it. It is a lot easier to define science than it is to say what spirituality is. Monks can puzzle over sub-atomic particles, but what should physicists use to supplement their learning? Are Gregorian chants, Tibetan prayer wheels and Jewish bar mitzvahs pretty much the same thing or must we choose among them?

The second problem is that spirituality changes slowly if at all, while science is constantly in motion. The writings of fourth century Tibetan scholars are significant to the Lama, but fourth century physics is only a curiosity. Science does not just add to accumulated knowledge. Sometimes it changes the rules of the game, and proceeds in an entirely new direction.

Reconciling science and religion isn't easy, but it is better than seeing the world with one eye closed.

# Almost Right or Totally Wrong

Sometimes being almost right is no better than being totally wrong. Any way you look at it, a near miss is still a miss.

There are no street lights in the condominium where we live. It would be dangerously dark, except for the yard lights each resident has. We all need to help keep the neighborhood safe.

A couple of weeks ago a neighbor told me that my yard light was burned out. I appreciated the warning. I didn't know it needed to be done since I never looked at the light at night. I replaced it promptly.

I was surprised to get the same reminder again yesterday. I fumed over the poor quality of bulbs that lasted only a few days. Then my wife remembered that we have two lights: one in front, one in back. I had replaced the front light. It was the back one that was burned out.

This is a disturbing thought. Some of the most important choices we make have to be completely right. If we tell the truth ninety percent of the time, that isn't good enough. A ten percent liar is still a liar. A husband or wife who is only mostly faithful is still unfaithful.

Most of us do good things most of the time. We're proud of that. We remember every generous gift to the victims of hurricane, flood, or earthquake. But we aren't always generous, don't treat everyone with kindness and courtesy, sometimes become angry or resentful or envious.

This is a religious problem. Faith should make us better, but it never makes us perfect. It is said that we are created a little lower than the angels. It is that little lower that causes a lot of the world's sorrows.

The notion that faith means being a nice person is naïve. None of us are that nice. Faith is not a reward for being nice. If we are good people most of the time, faith is the way we deal with the rest of the time.

The most important part of faith is forgiveness: not our forgiving, but our being forgiven. It is about the times we put the right bulb in the wrong light.

# Acquainted With Sorrow

One family member after another told me my car was strangely noisy. I didn't want to hear that, but in the end I had to agree. The mechanic didn't hesitate. Before we had driven a block he diagnosed a sickly wheel bearing. On a week with plenty of other problems I had to make room for one more.

This wasn't a good time for a misbehaving car. I was preparing for surgery. It was surgery I never wanted and hoped to never have. I had enough to think about.

There are a lot of things worse than automotive problems. Our health is more important than our cars. The people we love are more important than our money. There are a few great sorrows that never go away, but many daily distresses that burden our lives. That's all true, but it isn't a lot of help. Thinking about how things could be worse doesn't make little problems disappear.

There are times when our hearts are broken. There are also times when it seems we are being eaten by ants. Small problems wear us down even though they are trivial. Little problems heaped on more little problems tire the hardiest soul. Faith is not just the way we survive terrible blows. It is also the way we put up with a lot of nasty little annoyances.

That's what makes adolescence hurt so much. When we are young all problems are big ones. We have no large hurts to compare them with. We feel our life is in ruins and there is no hope for us. We must learn what great sorrows are before we can comfortably handle small ones.

An Old Testament prophet spoke of one who was "acquainted with sorrow." It is an odd turn of phrase. We can understand bearing sorrow bravely, of overcoming it with courage. But why should it be good to be acquainted with sorrow?

When we have been hurt we feel the hurts other people feel. A life of untroubled bliss would make us unfit to help anyone else. Even small sorrows soften our heart.

My car will be fine. I hope my surgery turns out that well.

# Does God Have a Business Plan?

Not long ago we bought things from people we knew. The clerk in the clothing store knew our name and the peculiarities that made our clothes hard to fit. The plumber who came in an emergency was someone we knew well enough to call at his home. Our prescriptions were filled by a pharmacist we knew and trusted. It was all very personal.

Now we buy things in Big Box stores, from people who know nothing about us and not much about what they sell. In an emergency we are shuttled to endless telephone menus, all of which have recently changed. What once was person-to-person is now number-to-number.

There are some good things about this. We have more choices of things to buy. The Big Box store offers hundreds of products that the corner store could never afford to stock. Prices are low, low, low because the only people paid to work in the store are stocking shelves or standing at the check-out counter. Nothing is personal, but everything is cost effective.

We buy from mass merchandisers and are entertained by mass media. Even our religion has given way to mass marketing. Faith, which was once our most intensely personal experience, is now the province of mega-churches. Success is defined as numerical growth, and no one questions that bigger is better.

The role of "pastor", once an honorable calling, is quaint and out of date. "Head of Staff" is the preferred title now.

Religion has always echoed the society in which it exists. It adopts the mannerisms of the day. In the feudal society the church was feudal, with Princes of the Church to match the princes of society. With the rise of democratic societies the church became democratic, with assemblies to make the rules and courts to enforce them. The institutions of faith have always been modeled on the secular institutions of their day.

Today power is not lodged in princes or legislatures, but in multi-national corporations. Accordingly, this is the day of the corporate church. It is cost effective and by its own standards, it succeeds.

One question is not answered. Does God have a business plan? Has the telephone menu changed?

# A Vicious Faith

Several young couples organized a baby-sitting co-op. It was partly to save money, but also they wanted their children to have the experience of playing in a group. It all worked quite well until they discovered that the husband in one family kept a loaded gun in their house. Alarmed at the thought of three-year-olds playing cowboy with live ammunition, the others expelled the offending couple.

They also wrote some rules: keep poisons out of reach of the children, lock up power tools, keep knives in a safe place. They discovered a surprising number of household objects are dangerous in childish hands. Usually they are useful. Sometimes they are lethal.

Religion is like that: wonderful at its best, but horrifying when it is abused. The juvenile notion that all belief is good doesn't take into account the kind of belief that straps on explosives and detonates them in a crowded market. Believing is not in itself good or bad. It is what you believe that matters.

Religion inspires the kind of sacrifice that leads to sainthood. It also motivates acts that lead to horrors. There is enormous power in faith. Sometimes that power is dangerous.

People readily admit that about other people's religion. The ancient Incas had worship practices that dismay modern minds. Head hunters and cannibals are clearly mistaken in their piety. We, of course, are different. We are too sophisticated for such crude practices.

That doesn't mean that we are never cruel in the name of God, don't shade the truth in our prayers, never cloak self-interest in claims of righteousness. Our faith doesn't always make us kind. Sometimes it doesn't even make us fair.

That's why there is no quarrel quite so vicious as a church quarrel. There is double hurt when a smiling villain claims to be doing the will of God. Words about love don't redeem unloving acts. They make them more painful.

People have denied the existence of God for centuries, and their denial hasn't done much harm. The real danger to faith is from those who know God exists and deny that God is good. The tears of those they hurt reveal the untruth of what they say.

# Saints are Rare, Politicians are Common

In ancient Greece it was believed that Delphi was the center of the universe. The famous Delphic Oracle issued strange prophesies. Peculiar gases seeped from the ground at Delphi. A few deep breaths of these fumes would lead to colorful insights into the future.

In more recent times certain citizens of the village of Philo, Illinois have claimed that their town is the center of the universe. This may have something to do with the Philo Tavern, a well-known Philo establishment. Although Philo is not as well known as Delphi it sounds like there might be Oracles there, particularly on Saturday nights.

Predicting the future is tricky, since the future soon comes and predictions are put to the test. That's why the writers of newspaper horoscopes become skilled in ambiguity. The trick is to make predictions so vague that no matter what happens it will probably fit.

A sudden change in fortune, for example, could mean either good luck or bad. It could also mean everything from winning the lottery to losing your billfold. I once was warned that my life would be changed by unexpected illness. It happened. My dog threw up on the living room rug, and I was late for an appointment because I had to clean it up.

One of the causalities of the information age is the business of making predictions. Predicting the economy or the next election or football games has to be done quickly. The outcome of he game, election or quarterly statistics will follow fast on the heels of our guesses.

The current fad in television reporting is to gather two or more professional prophets with conflicting views and let them shout at each other. Someone's prediction will be right because every possible outcome will be advanced by one of them. This generates a lot of heat but very little light.

When a politician begins a statement by saying, "With respect" you can be sure that the prophecy that follows will be most disrespectful. If they actually did feel respect for anyone they wouldn't need to announce it. Nobody ever said "With respect" when they were talking to Mother Theresa. Saints are rare, politicians are commonplace.

# Youthful Follies

The young man and his bride were being welcomed at a party given by his parents. When I congratulated them he remembered an incident from years before, when he was an adolescent. He had been temporarily kicked out of a youth group at the church, and I had come to his home to talk with him and his parents.

Someone asked what his offense was. I have no idea. What I remember was about myself, not him. When I went to his home I recalled that at his age I had been caught in some similar delinquency by Dr. Drake, the venerated pastor of my childhood church. Dr. Drake saw what I did, and I saw that he saw it. To my surprise he simply looked the other way. Neither of us ever mentioned it.

This no doubt colored my opinion of the boy, and kept me from thinking he was headed for a life of crime or depravity. If you work with teen-age boys it helps to be able to remember your own youth.

This made me wonder what the saintly Dr. Drake remembered that tempered his sense of justice. I had never thought about him that way before. I somehow imagined him incapable of adolescent follies. I thought he went right from infancy to a saintly crown, with nothing in between. When I think about it now this seems improbable.

What seems likely is that he was a perfectly normal boy. Adolescent boys do a lot of really stupid things. It is part of growing up. The combination of undeveloped judgment and surging hormones is as volatile as a terrorist bomb. Parents are lucky if their male heirs reach maturity without doing permanent harm to themselves or someone else. Dr. Drake's parents may have been lucky, but maybe not that lucky. He might have had a little youthful humanity to regret, like the rest of us. Maybe he remembered that.

Shakespeare wrote that "the evil men do lives after them, the good is oft interred with their bones." That may be true sometimes, but not always. Sometimes one good act endures, bouncing from generation to generation, like a ping pong ball on a stairway.

# What Computers Can't Do

We finished lunch, but the waiter couldn't give us a bill. All he could do was write down a lot of numbers, painfully add them up, and tell us the result. He explained that the computer was down. I hoped both his numbers and his math skills were up to the job.

Sometimes there's bad news that isn't anyone's fault. We just have to deal with it. This includes "The forecast is for rain, sleet, and freezing rain." It takes in a lot of unpleasant things a doctor may say to us. It also applies to that common disaster of the information age: "The computer is down."

When the computer is down everything comes to a halt. Letters can't be written, bills can't be issued, and records can't be kept or even accessed. Twenty years ago it wouldn't have been a problem. We had computers, but we hadn't become dependent on them yet.

Computers can remember things so complicated we have no hope of recalling them. They can make calculations that are not only accurate, but instantaneous. They can hurl messages across oceans and past the artificial boundaries between nations. They do so many things it is easy to think that they can do anything. They can't.

A computer can tell us what it will cost to buy a house. It can't tell us how to live in the house. A computer can remember a phone number. It can't tell us what to say when we call. A computer can analyze the chemical constituents of a human body. It can't distinguish between good and evil uses of our body.

A computer is useless for any decision that doesn't involve manipulating a mass of x's and o's. That includes most of the really serious questions. It can't answer the question "Does he love me?" or "Do I love him" or "What is the loving thing to do?"

In fact, it can't answer any questions that have to do with love, hate, generosity, sacrifice, evil or beauty. It can't answer questions that have to do with God. For that we need another language, another way of deciding, and another immeasurable kind of fact.

# A Lie is Still a Lie

I knew the last name of a doctor in Chicago. I wanted to know his first name and his phone number. From the Internet I learned all that and even saw a picture of him. (He has a beard.)

This is the Information Age. You can find out almost anything on the Internet.

What you can't always find out is whether the information is true. The doctor may have moved or have a new phone number. He might have shaved his beard. It is even possible that the web site I found is a work of fiction and no such person really exists. Anyone can put anything they want on the Internet, and they do.

There is a web site for every conspiracy theory and two for every hare-brained scheme to change the world. Technology is an open microphone where anyone can shout. It has no morals of its own, and it cannot discriminate between truth and lies. Technology is not a good thing or a bad thing. It can bless us or curse us. The choice belongs to the one who uses it.

A lie is a lie, whether it comes over a cell phone, is stored in a PDA, or appears on a monitor. It is the product not of the machine but of the human who lies. The newest technology does not create new heroes and villains. It only makes the old ones speak to a larger audience.

It doesn't really matter whether we use the latest tools to communicate. Some things can only be said by a still, small voice. What we say is altered by the way in which we say it. The words "I love you" mean one thing when they are whispered in a voice trembling with emotion. Publishing them to millions makes them mean something very different, something much smaller and less important.

We can speak to more people more often than ever before. When we do, we may not have anything to say.

The truth is still true, whether it is spoken on a Galilean hillside or published on a blog. Our hunger is not satisfied by the newest thing, but by the truest thing.

# A Dog's Best Friend

Of all the species on earth no two have bonded in quite the same way as the human and the dog.

When first a wolf-like creature peered at humans huddled around the fire outside their cave a relationship began. Gradually the dog conquered his fear and came close to pick up meat the human dropped. Before long the dog stayed and the human welcomed him. They warmed themselves by the same fire and shared the same food.

Dog owners sometimes say their canine thinks he is human. A scientist who knows about animals assures me this is not true. Your dog doesn't think he is human. He thinks you are a dog. You are not just any dog. The dog is a pack animal, and the dog's master is the leader of the pack.

This is not true of any other animal. A cat allows you to live with him if you behave, bringing food and water and doing the house cleaning. Horses bond to humans, but they are mostly useless as pets. Who wants to have a horse sit on their lap?

A dog wants to please the leader of the pack, and soon those primeval dogs made themselves useful. They herded the human's sheep, protected the human's home, and sounded the alarm at the approach of intruders. The dog guided humans who were without sight, and snuggled close to the human on cold winter nights.

Nothing makes a dog happier than serving his master. Nothing fulfills the dog like the praise of his human. An affectionate word and a pat on the head make the dog's life complete.

Dogs are not so much trained as set free to do what they are meant to do. Some breeds are herders and others are hunters. Some are guards and some are companions. They have some purpose deeply inscribed in their genes.

Humans are born with a purpose too. Like the dog, we are most fulfilled when we adopt the purpose we are meant to serve. We are here to serve our Master. Sadly, many drift through life aimlessly because they don't know what they are sent here to do.

What's inscribed in your genes?

# Changing the World Is Risky

The first place I saw a Red Hat Club was Eureka Springs, Arkansas. Eureka Springs is the kind of Ozark Mountain town whose sole reason for existence is to attract tourists. They feed tourists, sell things to them, and send them on their way.

A tour bus stopped in a parking lot in Eureka Springs. It disgorged a crowd of mature ladies, all wearing red hats. They quickly captured a restaurant, and after gathering strength they assaulted the souvenir shops like a conquering horde.

Now my mother-in-law has joined a Red Hat Club. The requirements for admission are not difficult but they are exclusive. A woman must have a red hat, a functioning digestive system, and a positive attitude toward life. The main activity of Red Hat Clubs is eating lunch. Their purpose is to have no purpose.

It is refreshing to find a group that doesn't try to change the world. These women don't take themselves that seriously. They are old enough to have tried changing the world, and they are willing now to just enjoy living in it.

There is no question that the world needs changing, and we have all benefited from groups in the past who were dedicated to changing it. Earnest joiners restricted child labor, slavery and the twelve hour work day, among other things.

But not every world-changing group has changed the world for the better. Some have given birth to vicious regimes on the left and the right. Hitler and Stalin and their earnest followers aimed to change the world. It would have been better if they had just bought red hats and had lunch.

People who are religious usually want to change the world. The record on that is mixed. Some very good changes have been fueled by religious enthusiasm. Democratic government and charitable enterprises of many kinds are expressions of religious faith. So are suicide bombers and racial or ethnic hatred. The strength of faith matters less than the nature of faith. Believing evil sincerely doesn't make it good.

Changing the world is serious business. There are two risks. The first is that we may fail. The second is that we may succeed.

# The Writing on the Wall

Sometimes something unexpected happens that brings a moment from your past vividly alive. What seemed ordinary at the time seems important when we remember it.

Many years ago we lived in a house on McKinley Avenue. We were a family: a mother, father, and two little girls (eight and ten years old). There were four bedrooms: one for the grown-ups, one for each of the girls, and one for guests. The girls chose the wallpaper for their rooms, violets for one and a colonial theme for the other.

Two other families have lived in that house since then. The family living there now is decorating, and they took off all the old wallpaper. They sent me pictures of what was revealed when the paper was taken away. On the wall of one bedroom was written in a childish scrawl "This is my bedroom" and a child's name, age, and grade in school. In the other room the other daughter's name was inscribed, along with her height and age.

When I saw those pictures I was remembered that long ago time, which seems like a kind of golden age now. I'm sure that it didn't seem that way at the time. There were problems that troubled me, disappointments that darkened the days. I don't remember them. That's one of the kindly gifts of memory. The joy lives on and the pain fades away. If that weren't true no mother would ever have more than one child.

When I e-mailed the pictures to the women who once were those girls they were unimpressed. One "vaguely remembered" writing on the wall, the other thought that perhaps her mother had done the writing. Neither was transported magically to a wondrous past. They live in the present, not the past. They are creating memories, not cherishing them.

We cannot however escape the past. We need not worship it but we should not erase it. You don't have to be a Jew or a Christian to know that the Ten Commandments have shaped the world we live in. No one's rights are infringed by acknowledging this fact. Celebrating the Ten Commandments will not convert anyone to being Jewish or Christian or even moral.

# Speaking for God

Copernicus made quite a stir in the fifteenth century. He wrote a book claiming that the sun is the center of our universe, and earth and all the planets revolve around the sun.

Everybody knew that the earth is the center, and that everything revolves around this planet. When Copernicus wrote the telescope hadn't been invented yet. Even gravity was no more than an idea waiting to be discovered. He didn't have much to work with.

Copernicus is a Latin name, but the man wasn't Italian. He wasn't even Copernicus. His real name was Mikolaj Kopernik, and he was Polish. In the fifteenth century people who went to college often gave themselves a Latin name. It was a kind of snobbery.

"Hey there! I'm Copernicus. I've been to college and you haven't. And by the way, the earth revolves around the sun."

Copernicus was right, but most people didn't care. They went right on farming and sailing ships and stealing from each other like they always had. In fact, most people had never heard of Copernicus, and hardly anyone knew about his ideas. His book wasn't published until just before he died, which saved him a lot of arguments.

He did however get tenure or something even better. He had an uncle who was a bishop, and he got Copernicus a job as canon at a cathedral. This provided him a comfortable income without having any duties, or even spending any time at the cathedral.

Copernicus' book prompted a lot of debate, even though he wasn't around to enjoy it. Most of the discussion was between men who also had Latin names. (No women were involved, this being before women were allowed in academia.)

Some of the arguers on both sides claimed that God agreed with them. They didn't deny that God made the planets move through the skies. The argument was about how God did it.

It's always risky to try to speak for God. God's ways are not our ways, according to the Old Testament. We've spent centuries trying to figure out exactly what God's ways are. It isn't easy. It's just as hard for Copernicus' heirs as it was for him.

# Shock and Awe at McKinley School

Palm Sunday marks the beginning of the Christian Holy Week. It is a solemn and awe-filled time for Christians.

In the past week I have heard the word "awesome" used to describe a salad dressing, a basketball player and a rock band. It is also used in regard to the Creator of the Universe.

There are two possible explanations for this. Either much of the population is in a constant state of awe or many people have never experienced awe and don't have a clue about what the word means. I think the second more likely.

Awe is more than applause. It is larger than respect. It is the sense of being in the presence of something immensely greater than we are.

A very long time ago I was a student at McKinley Grade School in Kokomo, Indiana. It would have been quite proper to call the principal, Mr. Sleeth, awesome. We were scared to death of him. Only the most incorrigible youths were summoned to his office. We didn't know exactly what Mr. Sleeth did to them there, and we didn't want to find out. That was truly awe.

No principal in this enlightened age wants to be feared by students. They want to be thought of as a friend, maybe even a buddy. It's not clear why a normal boy or girl would want a forty year old buddy with a weight problem. For that matter, it's unclear why a mature graduate of a College of Education would want to be a playmate with students. Isn't that what got Michael Jackson in trouble?

There is an element of fear in awe. We don't want to admit to feeling fear. It is symptomatic of low self-esteem, our most dreaded disease. It was once proper to speak of God-fearing men and women. It is most improper now.

A God who inspires fear is out of fashion. Today's God is more like a superior motivational speaker who makes us feel good about ourselves. This God inspires respect or admiration, but not fear.

When teachers are objects of derision and we worship an amiable deity, a really great pizza is indeed awesome. Whatever awesome means.

# My PDA Lost Its Mind

All the things I need to know are on my Personal Digital Assistant (AKA PDA). The PDA is a device smaller than a deck of cards that I carry in my pocket. It contains family social security and passport numbers, two versions of the Bible, my calendar of appointments, phrase books for French, German, and Italian, and all the addresses and phone numbers I use.

A few weeks ago it forgot everything. The battery ran down and the memory was wiped clean. There was a copy of all the information on my computer, but I couldn't find a way to put it back on the PDA. I also couldn't find the instruction manual that would tell me how to do it..

Everything electronic has an instruction manual. One of the first rules of the Information Age is that you must never lose the instruction manual. Whether it is changing a clock for Daylight Savings Time or adjusting the sound level of your telephone ring, you will need help some time. You can't solve these problems by reasoning. All electronic devices are unreasonable.

The current fad is electronics that do more than one thing. Cell phones take pictures and store music. Pocket calculators send and receive e-mail. Printers send faxes and make copies. By combining these functions you create the indispensable machine. When it breaks down you are totally helpless. You don't know anything and you can't do anything.

This kind of dependence is one definition of faith. Faith is trusting God for everything we know and everything we do. This is a splendid way to run your life. It is only possible because God always lives up to the responsibility. Trusting an electronic device this way is quite another matter.

The second rule of the Information Age is that anything you need to know is on the Internet. You may not know where it is, but it is in there somewhere. That includes the instructions for my PDA. I found it, and once again I have an electronic gadget that knows a lot more than I do. But I will never trust it quite as much as before. It is only a PDA.

# The Rest of the Story

The Christian holiday of Easter doesn't have much to do with rabbits or eggs, despite the games we play with our children. But what is it about? Exactly how does it affect our lives?

Easter is a response to some of the big questions of life. One of these questions is "Is this all there is?"

Are we like the dog in the children's poem?

"I had a dog. His name was Rover.

And when he died, he died all over."

Is life essentially pointless, Shakespeare's "tale told by an idiot, full of sound and fury, signifying nothing?" Can we really believe the Welsh hymn that says "truth alone is strong; though her portion be the scaffold and upon the throne be wrong?"

It sure doesn't look that way. Not in Rwanda or Darfur, not in all the killing fields across the ages.

The rain falls on the just and the unjust. Disease and natural disaster afflict all of us randomly. Truly evil people sometimes flourish. Good and gentle people often suffer. If the meek do inherit the earth, it's not where we can see it.

Easter is the most optimistic day of the year. It publishes the claim that this life isn't all there is. If that is the case it has enormous implications. It means that we see only a part of life, perhaps only a small part. Beyond what we see is a vast eternity, an utterly different reality that includes all of us.

Because there is more to life than we can see, all the unfinished stories can be finished. Good and faithful servants, unrewarded here, can enter into the joy of their reward. Those who suffer bravely suffer no more, and enjoy the freedom they hoped to find. Justice is completed, and truth finally triumphs.

Because there is more to life than we can see our life is purposeful and important. We don't just drift through existence to an ignominious end. We were born for a purpose, one that is uniquely ours, and it is up to us to find it.

Happy Easter! What happens in this world makes sense, if it's not all there is.

# The First Duty of A Politician

It's local election time. Cities, towns and villages are electing mayors and council members. Two promises are made by many candidates. One is to preserve the village (or town or small city) atmosphere. That's why many people moved there. The other is to promote growth. That's so the community will be more like the towns or cities where they chose not to live.

Nobody seems to see any conflict between these goals. It is our nature to hope that someone will find a way to eat the cake and still have it. Elections are won by candidates who convince people they can do that.

All political campaigns can be reduced to two stances. Incumbents point with pride. Challengers view with alarm. Neither is chastened by reality.

Democratic government is a blessing to all who enjoy it. It isn't heaven though, and every election reveals that. One side tries to gloss over unpleasant realities, while the other seeks to terrorize the populace with imaginary demons. It isn't a pretty sight.

It's a whole lot better than the alternative. If truth is abused in democracies it is slaughtered in dictatorships. It is not nice to lie about your opponents, but it is an improvement over shooting them. It is better to be afflicted with platoons of lawyers and press agents than by murderous secret police. Our system may not be painless, but it isn't evil either.

People who devote their lives to politics are not bad people. Most of them want to serve the public. They make considerable sacrifices in the effort. A candidate needs thick skin and a strong stomach. Campaigns inevitably include a lot of bad food and boring events, and a certain amount of plain nastiness.

The first duty of every politician is to be elected. If they don't do that nothing else matters. Capable, honest, public spirited public servants who win the election can make the world a better place. Capable, honest, public spirited losers don't achieve anything.

Some will win and some will lose in all these elections. Both the winners and the losers are sinners like the rest of us. No angels are on the ballot.

# Why Am I Here?

The world has a new Pope. There's a lot of speculation about what sort of Pope he will be. The best answer to that question is "Probably not what you expect."

Popes, like Supreme Court Justices, can't be fired and they can't be promoted. Unlike judges, they can't retire either. The Papacy is a life sentence, without the possibility of parole.

Popes don't have to think about opinion polls or the support of special interests. Popes are judged only by history and answerable only to God.

Very few people have this kind of freedom. This Pope never had it before. That makes it hard to know what he will do with it. It will all depend on what he thinks God wants from him.

We can know a lot about the Pope. What we can't know is what he prays about now. If we knew that we would know what to expect.

Most of us can be promoted, can be fired, and are not free to do what we want. We are pushed from every direction. We are answerable to our families, our friends, our employers, and the guy down the street who doesn't like dogs.

We get lots of advice, about everything. Nearly everyone wants to tell us something. Hardly anyone wants us to tell them anything. People we barely know have an opinion about us, for good or bad. We are judged daily by countless people. History won't notice us, but they will.

Despite all this, in the end we have to answer the same question the Pope must answer. God put me in this spot, with these relatives, this boss, and these neighbors. Why? What am I supposed to do here?

That's not an easy question to answer, for a Pope or for us. It is a question we can't afford to ignore or get wrong. Some very bad things have been done by people who thought they could read the mind of God. Equally bad things are done by people who don't care about the mind of God because they think their own mind is quite adequate.

Like the Pope, what we achieve will depend on what we pray.

# Savers and Throwers

There are two kinds of people. Some people save everything, including old power bills and their dog's rabies tag from last year. If they need anything they know they have it. They just don't know where it is.

Other people throw everything away promptly. They know where everything is, but it's too late to get it back.

Sometimes savers and throwers marry. In that case they both think they know where things are, but they're wrong.

This is one of the differences that nobody takes into account before they get married. In the enthusiasm of courtship no one asks if their beloved is a saver or a thrower. This is something they will find out soon enough.

That's the way it should be. The joy of marriage doesn't come from finding someone who is a mirror image of your self. It comes from the delight of discovering and accommodating to the differences. It is said that in marriage "the two become one." That doesn't happen magically at the end of the ceremony. It is the work of love that is long and constant.

That doesn't always happen. Maybe it never happens perfectly. It is a hope, not a certainty.

Paul writes in Corinthians that three things last: faith, hope, and love. Love is said to be the greatest of these, and everyone knows how important faith is. Hope doesn't get as much attention.

It should. We are never more than we hope to be. Hope makes the difference between accepting mediocrity and reaching toward perfection. We will not reach perfection, but we will reach farther than we would without hope. If we achieve all we hope, we have hoped too little.

Hope is the bright optimism that comes from faith and leads to love. We have hope because of our faith that the power behind the world is not our enemy but our friend. We dare to love others because our hope convinces us that we are loved. Hope is the confidence that life is good, when all the evidence we see is against it. Hope is the belief that dreams come true and on the other side of the troubled present is eternal goodness.

# Atwood, Illinois

Driving down a country road last week I passed a farm that was different from the usual corn and soy bean fields. A fenced in area held several dozen Shetland ponies. Nearby was another paddock with goats. I thought I saw a large animal that looked very much like a bison, although I'm not sure about that.

That's unusual, but not unique. One year when I made weekly trips to Indiana I often passed a field where llamas browsed. In our own county I have seen a farm from which giant birds, either ostriches or emus, stare at passersby. Better known is the nearby reindeer farm that advertises for visitors.

Since I have seen all these without trying, there are probably lots of places around here harboring exotic beasts. Clearly these farmers march to the beat of a different drummer.

We live in flyover country, that hidden part of America never seen by those who know only the East Coast and the West Coast. But there are people around here who live in drive-past country, invisible to those who never leave the Interstate highways. It is the American equivalent of the Cotswolds or Provence or Tuscany, rich in life that can't be seen in London or Paris or Rome.

We want to believe that most people are much like us. We're wrong. Most people are not only not like us, they are not like each other. That's why we need to get off the airplane and leave the highway.

We are a nation of micro-cultures. We are all similar, but not at all the same. We dream different dreams and dread different enemies. We define right and wrong differently. We aspire to different moralities.

Recognizing our differences doesn't mean that one dream is as good as another. That's not true. The world around us can bring out the best in us or the worst. Different definitions of a successful person make different kinds of success. Success on Long Island or Malibu terms is not the dream of people in Atwood, Illinois.

God created mankind, but the little worlds in which we live were not designed in heaven. That's something we did, for good or ill.

# Precious Ramotse

Botswana is a country in Africa, and that's about all most people know about it. It's all I would know if it weren't for Alexander McCall Smith. Smith is a Scot who was once a law professor at the University of Botswana. He writes books about that country.

Smith's books are not about the sadder side of life in Africa. They follow the life and friends of Precious Ramotse, who is proud of her country and thankful to live there. She is a "traditionally built" woman who pities the starvelings who count Atkins carbs or Weight Watchers points. She is an entrepreneur, the founder of the No 1 Ladies' Detective Agency.

Precious Ramotse has no doubt that "Botswana had to get back to the values that had always sustained the country and which had made it by far the best country in Africa." These values included "respect for age and respect for those who were traditionally built."

No reader will pity Precious Ramotse. Some will envy her.

Some people read a book because everyone else is reading it. That's not a good reason. Real readers read books they enjoy, not books other people enjoyed. Only one vote counts: yours.

Some books are really tools, not toys. They are serious books and they tell us how to do things or understand things. The pleasure we find in them is not an hour of distraction, but the ability to do something we want to do.

The Botswana books are not tools. We read them just for the fun of it. These books may make us wiser, kinder people or they may not. That isn't why we read them. At best they will make us enjoy a culture different from our own. At least they will warm our hearts and entertain us. Life is serious, but that doesn't mean that we have to be.

The ability to read is one of the richest gifts our Creator gave us. It gives us knowledge, but it also gives us fun. It is a gift too wonderful to be used only for serious things. Reading can make us happier, not just smarter. There are plenty of smart, sad people.

# Teacher Appreciation Week

If you were paying attention you had a chance this month to observe Teacher Appreciation Week. That's nice. Teachers deserve appreciation. You also could have celebrated National Women's Health Week and National Safe Boating Week. You could even have partied all month with National Bike Month.

If you missed any of those it's all right. There will be another round of special weeks next month. Anything that doesn't rate a week at least gets a day, like National Peanut Butter and Jelly Day. At least that's better than Abraham Lincoln and George Washington get. They only get a part of a day. We used to celebrate their birthdays, but now they have to share President's Day.

Bikes aren't the only cause that gets more than a week. Milk producers remind us of National Dairy Month. October is National Popcorn Poppin' Month, as though two different National Popcorn Days in January weren't enough. There's also a Vegetarian Awareness Month and a National Noodle Month. I don't know that I can think about noodles for a whole month.

All these special days, weeks and months have to compete with old fashioned holidays like Labor Day, Independence Day and Veterans' Day. Every religion has special holidays that are important to the faithful. Each person must remember certain days, like birthdays and anniversaries. (Some husbands forget one of these once. Only an idiot forgets one twice.)

We are fascinated by time. We measure it, count it, and name it. We worry about not having enough time. We get restless when we don't fill time. We put clocks everywhere so that we can know what time it is. We carry little books or electronic gadgets so that we always know what is supposed to happen at every moment.

We are stuck in the web of time, like flies in a spider web. We don't manage time. Time manages us.

If we think we just need more time we are mistaken. We need to escape from time.

Eternity isn't just a very long time. It is what we discover when all our time has been used up. In Eternity there are no special days. Maybe there aren't even any days.

# Life on the Brink of Reality

It's Cap-and-Gown time. The years of learning are coming to an end. Graduates linger on the brink of reality, and the voice of the Commencement Speaker is heard in the land.

It was at this season that Winston Churchill spoke at a college Commencement in Missouri. He told the graduates that an Iron Curtain had descended in Europe, giving a name to the division that would color more than half a century of history. His words would be echoed through decades of fear, danger and uncertainty. Most commencement speeches are not remembered that well.

They don't need to be. Commencement is not about the speaker, however important the speech turns out to be. It is about the graduates.

Even at that historic Missouri graduation, the audience was not really thinking about global politics. The graduates were thinking a little about what they were leaving behind, and a lot about what was ahead of them.

A major change was taking place in their lives. For some jobs were beginning and perhaps a marriage as well. Some would head for graduate school, a more serious business than undergraduate years. None of them could foresee with certainty where they would be in a few years.

For their parents pride was mixed with dismay. They felt suddenly older. Their own college years seemed barely over. Now their children weren't children any longer. Soccer moms were on the way to becoming grand moms. They were not comforted by the thought.

For the faculty the day was not quite so life-changing. One class was passing out of view. In the fall a new crop of freshmen would arrive. It was like the changing of the seasons.

Yet for the teachers as well as the students something was changing. They were a year farther from their own student years, and a year closer to retirement. They were a year wiser, a year more sophisticated, and perhaps a year more tired. There would be another new class in September, but it wouldn't be quite the same, and neither would they.

Commencement marks an important achievement by the graduates. It is a time of celebration and pride and joy. It is also pretty scary.

# Truth on the Dan Ryan Expressway

We started from the North Shore at 4 o'clock on a Monday afternoon. This was a bad decision. A flashing sign on the freeway told us it would take 47 minutes to get to the loop. It was an optimistic estimate. We were mocked by the 55-mile-an-hour speed limit signs. Much of the time we weren't moving at all. It took two hours to get clear of the city traffic.

Impatient drivers darted from one lane to another. They had forgotten the first rule of freeway traffic: the fastest lane is always the one you aren't in. There is no best way to drive during the rush hour. There are lots of worst ways.

While I impatiently drummed my fingers on the steering wheel I was degrading the environment, depleting a natural resource and further enriching the Saudi royal family. None of these are things I really want to do.

This is not an American phenomenon. There is so much traffic in London that they discourage people from driving in the central city by enforcing a special tax. Athens is as smog-bound as Southern California. China and India are now emerging from a long economic slumber and creating a middle class. The first thing the middle class wants is a car and a road to drive it on.

There is no such thing as a free lunch. Impatient hordes on the Dan Ryan are the price we pray for a life blessed by technology. There are still countries that can't afford a rush hour. Do I long for a simpler life, where only the rich and the tourists travel faster than a water buffalo? Don't be silly.

I want hot water for my shower, cool air on a summer night, and a chance to be with my grandchildren for their birthday or mine. I want a profusion of paperback books and all the imaging, antibiotics, and vaccines that make life longer and better.

I want music I can take with me. I want snapshots arriving on the internet. I want frozen waffles.

If the cost is rush hour traffic that is slower than a water buffalo, that's a price I can live with.

# We are Almost Geese

Our town is suffering from an avian population explosion. Canada Geese are on every pond and puddle. With my breakfast coffee I watched four families of geese walking through my side yard. They walk in a line with military precision. One adult leads the way, six or seven goslings follow, and the second adult brings up the rear, urging the stragglers on.

Canada Geese are handsome birds, but their sanitary habits are disgusting. They are pretty as they cruise on the water, but on land they foul every place where they parade. They are uncontrollable. A fence across our northern border wouldn't stop them. They not only can run and swim, but they can fly. They are the border patrol's worst nightmare.

Like the illegal immigrants from the South, they mean no harm and only want to improve their standard of living. Unlike those others, there is no one here anxious to hire them. Geese play no part in our economy.

These undocumented immigrants believe in big families. One pair of birds sneaks across the border, and soon they are a family of eight. By the third generation those two geese have filled the pond. That's when the wars begin. Feathers fly and squawks echo across the water, as two birds claim the same territory.

People sometimes say that a pet they love is almost human. In this case, humans are almost geese. Arabs and Jews have disputed the same land from the time of Abraham. In our country urban gangs mark their territory and battle with neighbors, while the affluent live in gated communities. Like the geese, many suffer but no one wins.

The greatest difference is that for all their screaming and fluttering, geese don't kill one another. They plant no bombs and never practice genocide. Humans are not so harmless.

I don't know if a Canada Goose would make a good Christmas dinner. I suspect that it would be illegal to try to find out. They are most likely protected, like owls and snail darters. They are not going to become extinct. If they start carrying the bird flu on their migratory flights ours may be the species that disappears.

# Angels along the Highway

There were many summers in my younger years when we drove from Illinois to the San Francisco Bay area. I was pursuing a doctoral degree, with more tenacity than skill. By the time I reached this elusive goal I had seniority over many in the faculty. In the end they had to either give me the degree or offer tenure.

We made these academic pilgrimages with a two door car, two small children and a dog. Besides the dog we took whatever lesser animals we owned at the time: turtles, frogs, and Siamese fighting fish. Since our stay was extended we also took a sewing machine, a small television set, and most of our possessions. A lot of these things were in a large plastic box that was clamped to the roof of the car.

Each time we traveled by a different route. We went south, through Amarillo, or north, through Calgary, or between through Reno and Cheyenne. We learned which motels accepted a dog and a traveling zoo, and which were close to national monuments, outdoor swimming pools, and child-friendly restaurants.

I learned one thing from these trips: How you make the journey matters as much as the destination you aim for. We always ended up in the same rented house in California and returned to the same home in Illinois. It was the adventures between that we remember.

There are good memories, like the first time our children saw tumbleweed tossed by the desert wind. There are not so good memories, like the high rise hotel in Los Angeles to which we can never return. (Descending from the tenth floor in an elevator with a vomiting dog guarantees that you will be remembered.)

We met angels. There was the Sunday in Banff when the car wouldn't start. We met a mechanic in church who opened his shop and got us on our way. We learned to enjoy the unplanned, like lunch at the Artichoke Capitol of the World.

Our life has been one long journey. We have been taken places we didn't plan to go and found pleasures we didn't know existed. It has all been good. It always will be.

# International Trade and a Virus

Maybe you're not worried about suicidal terrorists, tidal waves, mud slides or serial killers. There is something else you can worry about: chickens. Chickens could kill millions of people, destroy every economy in the world, and end civilization as we know it.

Or maybe they won't.

Disease control specialists live in dread of a virus that has been spread in Asia by birds. Wild birds carry the virus but aren't harmed by it. They give it to chickens which are killed by the virus, but may be the bridge to infecting mammals like us. If it is spread by humans the effect would be devastating. No country in the world is safe. No country is prepared for such an outbreak.

A hundred years ago nobody needed to worry about deadly diseases on the other side of the world. They stayed on the other side of the world. Today we are blessed with communication that has drawn the world together. China is just a jet flight away, and a lot of jets are flying.

The same technology that brings tee shirts across the Pacific can bring things that are neither planned nor welcome. Technology is both our blessing and our curse. When the world becomes a village, the whole village can get sick.

Nobody knows when or even if this will happen. What is known is that it could, and that if it does it will be devastating. It will be a doomsday pandemic. We will all be victims, not of a nuclear holocaust, but of a humble virus.

There has always been speculation about the end of the world. Ignoring the Biblical injunction that nobody can know when the world will end, some have been bold enough to predict the date. Until now they have all been wrong.

We don't need to know when the world will end. We can be sure that for us it will end in a measurable number of years. We will all die, if not all together, then surely one by one.

The real question is not when the world will end. It is what will come after the world ends, whether for you and me or for everyone.

# Old Wars and Forgotten Victories

There are days that mark a turning point in our lives, though often we don't recognize them until long after. Many of them are about decisions we have to make: about a marriage, about a job, about where we shall live or how we shall pay for the living. But other turning points are not made by us. They are presented to us, and we must deal with them.

Losing a job or a mate or a friend is like that. I suppose that winning a lottery is like that, too. Sudden, irrevocable changes are always a challenge, and the good ones challenge no less than the unwelcome.

Movie stars, sports stars, and entrepreneurs can suddenly come into unbelievably large amounts of money, more in a year than most people earn in a life time. Some fail to pass the test, and their lives are ruined by good fortune. They can begin to believe that they are not like other people, and that they deserve to be rewarded richly. That's a road that can lead to destroyed families, or sometimes to a federal prison.

Most of us are spared this kind of test, though we would be willing to try. Publishers Clearing House and the Readers' Digest don't come to our door. We don't even buy lottery tickets. We have no talents that can be extravagantly rewarded.

Our challenges are more likely to be ones we wouldn't choose. The mere process of aging is a challenge. It comes as a surprise, an unnoticed day at a time. We can't believe that we are as old as the calendar insists, until suddenly we realize that our memories are better than our expectations. That is something we cannot change or escape.

It is a time to savor those memories, and be thankful for them. There were dangers we escaped and hurts we survived. There were friendships that warmed cold days, and victories that most have forgotten. We are the veterans of old wars and the builders of crumbling buildings, but the glory has not faded.

We believed that behind all the changes was an unchanging love. We were never alone in those times.

We aren't alone now.

# Self-Inflicted Crimes

The police are waging war against people who don't put their seat belts on when they're in their cars. "Click it or ticket" is the slogan of the crusade against the great unbelted masses. We will all be safer soon, whether we want to or not.

This doesn't affect me. I put on my belt without thinking. Once many years ago I turned a car over, end over end, with my elderly mother seated beside me. We were safely belted in and neither of us was injured. Since then I have been a true believer in seat belts.

I shudder when a motor cyclist without a helmet breezes past me. I have visited his fellow dare devils in the hospital wards, struggling to regain the use of unresponsive arms and legs. In some states riding without a helmet is legal, in some it is not. It risks horrible consequences everywhere.

These are not victimless crimes in any state. The victims are also the perpetrators. The crimes inflict their own penalties, far harsher than those of courts.

Self-inflicted crimes go beyond those recognized in law. The penalty for repeated lying is the loss of trust. The penalty for unfaithfulness in marriage is the loss of that complete trust that is the crowning glory of a union. The penalty for greed is the surrender of self-respect as well as the respect of others.

The Ten Commandments could equally be called the Ten Warnings. They are not bureaucratic regulations set forth to trap us. They are danger signs, protecting us from the injuries we can do to ourselves. Failing to honor parents or to be faithful to vows deprives us of happiness we ought to enjoy. False gods deprive us of the real God. In every self-chosen failure there is a self-inflicted punishment.

How many lies does it take before nobody trusts your word? What part of "you shall not bear false witness against your neighbor" don't you understand?

The legislature can't list every dangerous thing we may choose to do and set fines for it. They are bound to miss a few. What the legislature overlooks will be punished in the emergency room.

# The Sea Sick Romantic

When I was growing up all my relatives were either immigrants or the children of immigrants. The older generation came, pursuing their dream of a prosperous life in the New World.

All that is except one: my Uncle Gideon, the husband of my father's sister, Hilma. Uncle Gideon was a quiet, gentle man. He was also an illegal immigrant.

He had a more romantic dream. He wanted to see the world, to ride in the rickshaws of Hong Kong and hear the call to prayer in Istanbul. He went to sea, signing on as an apprentice sailor on a ship sailing from his native Copenhagen.

There was a flaw in his plan, and he knew it before the ship was out of the harbor. Before they were properly at sea he was hanging over the rail, retching and heaving. With glazed eyes and trembling hands he went about his seaman's duties as well as he could, which was not very well. He yearned to be on dry, stable land.

At New York he got off the ship. He wrapped his arms around the first stable object he saw, and took one look back at the ship that was the source of all his suffering. Then he turned and walked away as quickly as he could. He did not go to Ellis Island, or any other entry point for immigrants. He headed inland.

In Chicago he found a job in a company that packaged and sold cheese and butter. He acquired a Dodge automobile, a house in Chicago's Rogers Park and Aunt Hilma, although not necessarily in that order. He achieved the dream, but it wasn't his dream.

The one thing he couldn't acquire was a voter's registration card. In Chicago people sometimes vote after they die, but no one votes before they are citizens. To become a citizen he would have to return to Denmark, get a visa, and make still another transatlantic crossing. Just thinking about it made him nauseous.

Uncle Gideon learned early something we all learn sooner or later. No matter how carefully we plan, God's plan may be quite different.

# How Am I?

Sickness is like a gaseous substance. It expands to fill the available space. That is not a function of the seriousness of the illness. It is as true for the summer flu as for full-blown AIDS. When you are sick, it is hard to think of anything else. It fills your life.

It was true of Dr. Hurd Allyn Drake. He was the pastor of my youth, who influenced my life more than anyone save my father. I visited him in what proved to be his last illness. I expected him in such serious straits to talk about the meaning of life and death, about faith in the hardest of hard times. Instead he gave me detailed accounts of fevers and drugs, discussed in intimate detail bodily functions I did not want to think about. His life had closed in around his failing body, leaving no room for anything else.

When you are sick people will invariably ask how you are. They do not mean the question to be taken clinically. They are not interested solely in your embattled body. You are much more than that.

They want to know about the whole you, about your mind and spirit and faith. That much you can at least partly control, when there is so much that you can't. Your body reminds you that you are mortal. Your faith insists that you are more than blood counts and weakened flesh.

Your friends who ask about you remind you that it is not all about you. Their world goes on as it did before. Children still play, the young fall in love, and those in their middle years still pay too much for gasoline and worry about the next election.

People still pray, and not always about you. You still pray, and not only about yourself. There is still music to hear and jokes to tell. There is still a world outside your skin, and you are still a part of it.

The question is, do you have a problem or does the problem have you?

How am I? All in all, I'm pretty good. That's an honest answer. Anything else is only part of the truth.

# The Entrepreneur and the Terrorist

In most countries the best way to become rich is to choose the right grandparents. If they are wealthy, you probably will be too. If you are born in poverty you will probably stay poor, and your children need hope for nothing better.

America is the Land of Opportunity. We believe in the Horatio Alger myth. A poor boy or girl works hard and becomes wealthy. The amazing thing about this story is not that we believe it. It is that it actually happens. Great corporations begin in a basement or garage or a college dorm room. They succeed immensely, and the children of ordinary parents become the parents of wealthy children.

When this happens we all want to know the secret of their success, and they oblige by giving speeches or writing a book. It is usually the same speech or the same book. They all know the same secret.

The secret is to be committed to success. Believe in yourself. Believe in what you are doing. Stay focused on success, even when failure seems certain. Work harder than everybody else. Never give up. Those who are most committed achieve the most.

It's easy to describe, but very hard to do. Success did not drop on them from the sky. They clawed their way to it. They were willing to sacrifice everything to reach their goal. The secret of their success is no secret at all. It is simply commitment to success and the willingness to pay what it costs.

Positive thinking, personal sacrifice, and unrelenting effort are the way a billionaire is made. They are also the way unworthy goals are reached. Nobody sacrifices as much or tries harder than a terrorist. The same attributes that lead to creating Microsoft can lead to a suicide bombing.

Commitment is the key to great achievement, whether for good or for evil. A half hearted commitment to success will lead to half a success. But commitment itself is not good. It depends on the cause to which you are committed.

Both the entrepreneur and the terrorist are committed to what they do. The same commitment that is a blessing in one is malignant in the other.

# Klunks

My car made an unusual sound as I turned a corner. There are a lot of usual sounds, but this one was different. It sounded sort of like "klunk". On the next corner, there was another klunk. On every turn I heard the same sound.

I think my car made this kind of noise once before, and it turned out to be important, although I don't remember why. I drove to the dealership, where a mechanic offered to go on a test drive with me. Apparently he wasn't familiar with klunks.

You can probably guess the rest of the story. The car refused to klunk. We drove around the block; we drove in circles around an abandoned parking lot. Finally the mechanic, who was a kind man and a diplomat, said he once had to drive a car three days to get it to make the sound a customer complained about. He told me the next time it made the noise to come back and we would test it again.

It hasn't klunked since.

I don't think the car's return to normal sounds was an answer to prayer. I don't pray about car klunks. That's not because I doubt God's power, but because it isn't a car-sized problem. Praying about such things would be like asking an orthopedic surgeon to trim my toe nails.

I don't doubt God's power to silence car noises and heal automotive illnesses. That's the definition of God: the one with power over everything. What I doubt is my knowledge of how God will use that power in any given circumstance.

It's true that God sees the sparrow that falls, but the Almighty doesn't pick up every fallen bird and put it back in the next. For the most part sparrows are on their own, subject to the laws of gravity and mortality. So are we.

# Good Gifts and Hard Times

My computer, which sometimes does things I don't understand, suddenly shut down its monitor. That's the screen that is the only way it communicates with me. Nothing I tried would turn it on again. Then it started working, with no more warning than before it quit. It's working now, but there is a difference. I don't trust it.

I never thought about the monitor, but I think about it now. It failed once, and I am waiting for it to fail again. Something was lost in that brief failure. I can never trust it as confidently as I did before.

Our lives are built on trust, and the loss of trust is serious. When trust is lost, in a marriage or a business partnership or a profession, the whole relationship is threatened. Trust can be lost quickly, but once lost it isn't easily brought back. Apologies and promises aren't enough. To believe them we have to have trust, and that is what we have lost.

Trust is not belief in what a person says. It is belief in who they are. Trust is the confidence that they do not change or deceive or betray. Someone who is truthful most of the time is a liar part of the time. There is no way to be certain which time can be trusted.

Trust in God is not about what God says or does, but about who God is. Trusting God is being sure that God is on our side, the same yesterday, today and forever. We can't predict what will happen to us.

Sometimes terrible things take us by surprise. The doctor may give us bad news, we may lose our job, someone we depend on dies or betrays us. Our faith won't protect us from those things. When it rains everyone gets wet, whether they have deep faith or none at all.

Regardless of our faith we will enjoy happy times and endure sadness. We will be blessed more than we deserve, and rewarded with more than we have earned. Trust is not about whether we are blessed or suffer. It is about how we receive good gifts and survive hard times.

# A Celebrity in a Yellow Shirt

Aspen, Colorado is a ski resort in the winter. In the summer music is its main attraction. A symphony orchestra performs under a canvass tent. Outside is the beauty of the mountains. Under the canvass there is another kind of beauty, expressed in glorious sound.

On an August afternoon a murmur spread through the crowd. A well known movie star was in the audience. At least, the whisper that went through the crowd said that's who he was. Thoughtfully he wore a bright yellow shirt, so it was easy to identify him.

When the last chords died down there was a hushed pause, as the crowd returned from the beauty of the performance to the every day world. In that brief moment the famous man rose, walked quickly to the podium and shook hands with the startled conductor. Then the man in the yellow shirt strode down a side aisle and out of the concert tent. The crowd, still seated, watched him leave.

That was my brief brush with celebrity or at least with a man in a yellow shirt. Films create their own kind of fame. Its high achievers are recognized everywhere they go. They are as rich as oil sheiks, showered with praise at the countless award ceremonies the industry provides for its own self-congratulation..

Unfortunately some of them confuse their celebrity with brilliance. They consider themselves qualified to advise commoners on politics, religion and economics. They freely express their opinions on subjects about which they know less than the ordinary citizens they despise.

This kind of conceit is not confined to actors. Fans think they are smarter than coaches, and some shout profane advice at ball games. Teachers who know more than the rest of us about their subject occasionally wax oracular about things outside their competence.

The clergy are particularly generous with their wisdom. When religious scholars try to run a country the result can range from tragic to ludicrous. The Taliban was tragic, but Americans have their own examples of clerical meddling. Prohibition was an absurd response to the disaster of alcoholism.

We are each created for a purpose, great or small. The trouble begins when we want s bigger role.

# Second Place Winner

When I was a student there was a preaching competition among the seminaries in Chicago. I didn't win, but I remember a line from the sermon of the man who did. He said that he didn't want to "serve up half a Christ for those with tender minds... a palatable capsule that shallow people can swallow with ease."

That was a worthy goal, and if he came close to reaching it he deserved to win. There are a lot of shallow people, and it is a temptation to seek their approval by making things easy for them. Religious careers have been built on less.

Of course, no minister would admit to serving up a fractional faith, even to himself. In fact, every minister I've ever known thought he (or she) was a pretty good preacher. That's not conceit. How could they think otherwise? People line up every week to tell them they did a great job. They can't all be lying.

What else can a departing worshiper say except that it was a good sermon? It's either that or the weather, and the person before you probably covered that.

George Buttrick, who was a preacher in New York, collected some of the strange things that people said to him as they left church. His favorite was "Reverend, every sermon you preach is better than the next." A close second was "That sermon was like a glass of water to a drowning man."

It seems strange that we should judge the piety of religious professionals by their ability to interest a crowd of drowsy people on Sunday morning. Some are pretty good: a touch of humor, a little pathos, maybe a few lines of poetry. Make them laugh, make them cry, quote somebody famous. It's not exactly Pulitzer Prize material.

It's not the skill of the speaker that matters most. Any sermon is good if it is sincere. At its best it is one person sharing his faith with another. It doesn't need to be pretty. It just has to be true. Polished hypocrisy is not redeemed by its literary value. The truth is always worth hearing. Lies are not improved by eloquence.

# Desperate Housewives, and Other Losers

The current fad in television is portraying dysfunctional families. The housewives are all desperate, the brothers and sisters lie to one another, and it's not clear who the father is. Every family has its obligatory homosexual, its despised bigot, and its weepy neurotic.

It wasn't always like that. Once television dads called out "I'm home, honey" as they came in the house, suited and necktied. Honey, not a hair out of place after a day of baking cakes and pies and making clothes for the entire family, beamed a smiling welcome. The children, all polite and obviously loved, waited for Dad to give sage advice for their minor problems.

It wasn't real, of course. Even the actors didn't have families like that. They were as likely as others in Hollywood to substitute serial polygamy for family life. Their children were already practicing for their tell-all books on the failures of their parenting.

The two pictures of family life are equally false. Real families don't communicate freely and comfortably. Parents commonly don't have any idea what teen-agers are thinking. Most adolescents go through a silent phase when they speak mainly in monosyllables.

On the other hand, the lack of communication doesn't always mean that dark secrets are being hidden. It doesn't even mean that everybody is talking and nobody is listening. I am frequently surprised at how much I remember that my parents said, even though at the time my only response was "Whatever."

Of course there are families that are shockingly bad and others that are very, very good. Both extremes are rare. Most families are neither as good as we hope nor as bad as we fear. Most have times of sheer joy and times that tear our hearts. In the end most families will be remembered for their happiness, not their struggles.

That we are entertained by accounts of disastrous families and not by impossibly good ones tells a lot about us but very little about family life. In that Ozzie and Harriet era we dreamed of what we wished our families were. Now we are encouraged by knowing that our families are a lot better than the ones on television.

# Laws of God and Men

New occasions bring new crimes. Identity theft is the new crime of the Information Age. A generation ago crooks had to be satisfied that stealing your money or your property. Now they can steal you.

We have some protection. At least, I think we do. Every few weeks brings another promise to protect my privacy. They come from my doctor, my banker, my insurance company, even my pharmacist. I get one from everybody who has any dealings with me or my money or my health. They all arrive in the same fashion: several pages of dense type, a format that begs not to be read. I don't read them.

I hope they say something like "We won't tell anything we know about you to anyone else without your permission." Maybe they do. Since I have never read any of these privacy statements, let alone all of them, I don't know.

Although these privacy policies are addressed to me, they aren't written to me. They are written by lawyers, to other lawyers. There is a smell of the courtroom about them. They are written in Legalese, a language as unintelligible as Sanskrit to most of us. They are not written to communicate, but to be used in court.

That is the nature of laws  No law is ever perfect. Some have effects no one planned. Some offer loopholes that cam be exploited by clever malefactors. Some even have the opposite effect than what was intended. A good law punishes most of the guilty appropriately and treats most of the innocent fairly, but not always or in every case.

The Ten Commandments are sometimes held up as the Law of God. The difference between that law and ours is not that God is a better lawyer. It is in what laws are intended to do.

The laws enforced by our courts are intended to punish harmful behavior. The moral laws of faith are intended to warn us that harmful behavior is dangerous. The punishment is the result of our harmful acts. The Law of God aims not to punish us, but to tell us how to avoid the punishment we can inflict on ourselves.

# What We Have and Who We Are

It is one thing to be in a winter storm in the Middle West. It is quite another thing to read about it on a nice day in Florida. You're bound to feel a little guilty about basking in the tropical sun while the hostages you left behind are coping with life in blizzard country. Like the rain, snow falls on the just and the unjust. Nobody deserves it.

Some bad things we bring on ourselves, and we should feel guilty. Some are done to us by other people, and they should be ashamed. Some just happen, they are nobody's fault, and nobody is guilty. They are part of living in this unruly world.

There is no sure connection between our blessings and our deeds. Everybody, good or bad, gets the same weather and suffers the same diseases. The best people sometimes die unrewarded and the worst may live to savor the harvest of their evil.

It isn't fair. Life is unfair.

One of the ironies of creation is that the human, the only creature to know the difference between right and wrong, is the one who must see the unfairness of life. We know what justice is, and we know that sometimes it comes too late.

Saints die unnoticed before their dreams are fulfilled. Bloody-handed dictators persist in their depredations. Many lives end as unfinished stories. We want to know the rest of the story.

The most important question we can ask is, "Is this all that there is?"

That same human, able to know good and evil, is able to conceive of good and evil too large to be completed in this universe. From the most primitive humans to those living now they have sought to see the invisible and expect universes beyond the one in which they lived. That is how they learned to pray.

We search for meaning in life. We want to know that it is better to reject temptations than to give in to them. We want to know that it is better to give than to take. We want to know that what we have is good now, but who we are is good forever.

# Please Enter Your Pin

We have an alarm system at our house. It makes me nervous. I breathe a sigh of relief whenever I complete a transaction with this device. One mistake and I have to explain my failure to the local police. They are too polite to tell me that I am an idiot, but they don't congratulate me either.

I feel the same way about putting my debit card in an ATM machine. I have to enter a number called a PIN. If you do it wrong you can try again, but not several times. The suspicious machine will refuse to give the card back if you make too many wrong guesses. I did that once in Portugal. You can imagine the problem of straightening that out with bank clerks who only speak Portuguese.

Today we have passwords for almost everything. We are told to change them frequently, but never write them down. Use last week's password and you're locked out. You have to remember the right password for the right purpose, and it's not what it was the last time you used it. Can anybody really do that? I can either change the password or remember it, but I can't do both.

We use PIN numbers and passwords to keep people from stealing our identity. The trouble is that if our identity isn't stolen we may misplace it ourselves. Nobody else will be able to take money out of our checking account, but we won't either. A misplaced identity isn't as expensive as a stolen one, but it is still a nuisance.

When our city was a small town this wasn't a problem. There weren't any machines that you had to satisfy. You went in the bank to get money, and the people there knew who you were. That meant you had to go to the right bank at the right time. I couldn't get money from strangers in a Florida bank, let alone at midnight on the street in front of the grocery store.

The trouble with modern society isn't just that it is impersonal. It may make it hard to know which person we are. Without a PIN we are nobody.

# How Do You Define Success?

College athletes often appear on television after a game. Having a microphone thrust in your face and being asked how you feel about the game your team just lost is not a lot of fun. Even those enrolled in the College of Communications aren't at their best at such moments.

They tend to say the same things. They're going to "play one game at a time", they need to "take care of business". It's probably an echo of their coach's locker room oratory.

It's not surprising that athletes should consider a business model for their sport. That's the current fad. Universities are no longer ivy covered sanctuaries of scholarly pursuits. An accountant who audited several universities described one approvingly as "like a Fortune 500 corporation." Not-for-profits keep an eye on the bottom line even more than on the target of their efforts. Mega-churches are proud of their business plans. Athletes are no different.

The question is, "What kind of business did the coach have in mind?"

Probably not the Ford Motor Company, desperately thrashing on the brink of bankruptcy. Certainly not Enron, disgraced and discredited. But there are others. Maybe they're thinking of Google or Yahoo.

I once visited a business in our town. It was an aggressively casual company. Employees wore jeans and sweat shirts, not suits. The building had once been a school, and it included a gymnasium. This was an asset, because people working there could take a break by shooting baskets or playing impromptu games.

The CEO was honored as the State Entrepreneur of the Year. I asked him exactly what it was that his high-tech start-up made. He thought for a moment before he replied, "I know what it doesn't make. It doesn't make money."

That wasn't its goal. Its goal was to develop an idea and turn it into a product. That product, which I still don't understand, was only a dream until someone showed it could be useful. That was a job for men in jeans, not accountants.

Eventually the company was bought by a larger corporation and moved out of town. There are government offices in the building now. I hope they play basketball.

# Reality That Isn't Real

Reality television is the latest twist in small screen entertainment. It consists of shows with no actors, no writers, and very little plot. Reality shows are fascinating because they show a desperate conflict. It's like watching a dog fight.

There are two types of reality shows. Both are exciting because there is conflict between contestants. The first kind brings together a large group of people to compete for a lot of money. Only one of them will win. They are put in unpleasant places and required to do disgusting things. The winner is the one who can outsmart and outlast the others.

This is almost realistic. In the real world the winner would be the one who murdered everybody else. This is how dictators win a whole country. The legal departments of the networks forbid this obvious route to success.

The other type of show motivates the contestants with sex as well as greed. The prize is not only money but marriage. Money is still involved though. It is necessary to find someone the contestants would want to marry on little or no acquaintance. This must be a person who is physically attractive and personally charming. Having the money to offer a glamorous life style is a great help. It would be hard to find a group of attractive women who would fall all over one another to win a proposal from the bag boy at the supermarket.

Girls do of course fall in love with bag boys, marry them, and live happily ever after. They just don't do it on television. It's not the stuff dreams are made of.

Reality shows are eagerly watched because they offer both suspense and gratification. Nobody knows who will win, but everyone knows who should win. You can't watch for long without having a favorite, someone who, if there is any justice in this world, ought to win. When that happens you aren't just watching a dog fight. You have a dog in the fight.

That's the difference between faith and religion. Faith is religion made personal. It is when you don't just know about God and good and evil. You have a dog in the fight.

# Snakes and Doves

Jesus was one of the few people to say a good word about snakes. He told his disciples to be "as wise as serpents and as gentle as doves." We're pretty good at the wise part. We produce more engineers, physicists and MBA's than any country in the world. We know how to make things fast and cheap and sell them to everybody.

Even our charities are efficient. They solicit money expertly and carefully calculate how to get the most contributions for the least investment. The missionary who tours churches to tell about far places and show his souvenirs is out of date. His successors use PowerPoint.

Underneath our modern skills there is a certain unattractive ruthlessness. In both business and non-profit enterprises there is often a struggle to control the rewards of success. The competition that spurs prosperity can be a temptation to win by any means. A little exaggeration is good advertising. Too much is a lie. Does anyone really believe the claim that a product is "new and improved?"

Advances in medicine have limited suffering and postponed death. They have also tempted athletes to seek drug-induced victories. We can publish our thoughts cheaply and send them instantly to the corners of the earth. That works for incitement to hatred as well as for ordinary commerce.

Everyone who uses Email has heard from a Nigerian woman whose deceased spouse has left a large sum of doubtfully acquired money in a Swiss bank account. This is a double dose of misuse of technology. It is both an appeal to our cupidity and a simple case of fraud.

When we can do anything we want to do, the question of what we want is the important one. What we want is simply to win, to scoop up the marbles and let the losers pay the price.

There is not much kindness in our business-like world. We are quite willing to use our skills to play hardball. The hands that pick up the trophy are too often soiled from the contest we won.

Jesus told his disciples that being as wise as serpents is not enough. We must also be as gentle as doves.

# Living in a Dangerous Neighborhood

Last week our neighborhood drug store had a new clerk. She was a pretty young woman. She smiled at customers as she scanned their purchases and gave them credit card receipts to sign. She made them feel welcome. She wore a scarf on her head, a sign that she was a Muslim.

North of town a group wants to build a temple. We call our places of worship churches, unless we are Jewish. These pious people are not Jewish. They are Hindus, who want to build a Hindu temple.

We have come a long way. Protestants, Catholics and Jews are friends and neighbors in our Midwestern town. We never expected to have neighbors whose styles of worship we have only seen in the pages of the National Geographic.

Not long ago other faiths were far away in exotic corners of the world. We only encountered them when we were tourists and they were the quaint people we visited. Now they live next door.

Welcome to the twenty-first century.

It is a century in which differing faiths cannot avoid one another. Hindus hate and fear Muslims, Muslims hate and fear Christians, and everybody hates the Jews. Sometimes we even hate and fear those most like ourselves: Protestants and Catholics, Sunni and Shia, or Baptists, Methodists and Presbyterians whose churches divide.

It is a dangerous century, awash in spiritual danger. On the one hand we risk losing our faith, melding all religion into an innocuous mush. On the other hand we risk being taught to hate, to deal with other faiths as though they are a threat we must defeat at any cost.

When the world has shrunk to a neighborhood, how do we live together without killing one another?

For the atheist the answer is simple: get rid of religion, all religions. It is not so easy for the vast majority who live and find happiness in their faith. Losing that is a too great a price to pay.

In the end, every question is a theological question. This is the one we can no longer avoid. It cannot be solved in 350 words, or in 350 thousand words. It is the question that could destroy us.

# A High School Graduation

High school graduation means a lot of very different things to the very different graduates. For some it is just a milestone on a longer journey. There was never any doubt that they would reach it. The only questions were about how good their grades are and what schools they can move on to. Not graduating is simply inconceivable.

For others graduation is a victory, a prize won overcoming forces that stood in their way. At a high school commencement I saw recently there were two students pushed in the processional in wheel chairs. Others had endured the derision of friends. Some had no model of success, no support in their home. Some had struggled to learn what most understood without much effort. From birth their future was in doubt.

Our lives are not determined solely by how hard we try or even how gifted we are. Things we can't control set the boundaries of our life. Just the fact of being born in the United States or in Bangladesh or the south of France makes a difference. It is not the only difference, but it is important. It determines what opportunities we have.

Our lives are a series of opportunities, different for each of the students at that graduation. (And also for the others who had the opportunity to graduate, but did not.) We cannot control which opportunities are set before us. We completely control what we do with those opportunities.

The graduates file solemnly in, while the high school band plays Pomp and Circumstance. The band plays the tune again and again, the graduates all wearing the same academic gowns, all walking to the same stately beat. But each one is different, dealing with different opportunities, coming from different beginnings, heading for different lives. Each is important, but in different ways. Each has an opportunity to make the world complete. Each can do what they choose with that opportunity.

Like all of us, each graduate can succeed or fail. Success has a different meaning for each of us. It is success at making the best of our opportunities, whatever they are. It is being the best at what God intended us to be.

# Choose Your Own Idiocy

If you don't want to listen to Fm or AM radio, a CD, or an MP3 player, you don't have to endure silence in your car. There is still satellite radio.

Ordinary radio comes from a single station somewhere close to where you are. If you don't like what that station is broadcasting you can tune to a different station, or wait until the program ends and another one begins. Satellite radio comes from the sky and offers more than a hundred stations, each sending out a different kind of programming. If you want jazz, there are three or four kinds. If you want news, there are three or four varieties.

Satellite radio is almost everything. It can be heard anywhere. Well, almost anywhere. If you are on the north side of a building it may not work. It has no commercials. Well, almost no commercials. There are no commercials on music channels. With any program that involves speaking you are fair game to advertisers. It is free. Well, almost free. When you buy a car with a satellite receiver it is free for a while. Then you either pay up or they shut it off.

Ordinary radio claims to be unbiased. To prove this they sometimes bring together two or more people who are violently committed to different points of view. They shout at each either, interrupt each other, and question one another's sanity. Everybody has an equal opportunity to act like an idiot.

Satellite has similar spokespersons, but they put them on separate channels. That way you can choose the idiocy you prefer and listen to it unadulterated.

Satellite radio gives the listener a lot to choose from, whenever the listener wants it. It answers our demand for instant gratification. We want what we want, and we want it now. Satellite gives it to us.

The trouble with instant gratification is we can't get some of the best things that way. Some things – love, integrity, the satisfaction of a useful life – are earned by long commitments, faithfully kept. For those things we need patience and the willingness to wait. Some times the best sound is no sound at all.

# Aging Begins When We Are Born

This spring a nursery school observed its Graduation Day with a Toddler's Commencement. A dozen little kids were draped in tiny robes and mortarboards. They wandered about the room, more or less in step to the recorded strains of Pomp and Circumstance. The children were as cute as all get out, and it was a great photo op for parents.

About the same time a Middle School announced that it would no longer hold the annual graduation ceremony. Apparently adolescents don't rank as high as kindergartners on the cuteness scale.

Honoring little ones who get an A in coloring inside the lines is one thing. Finishing high school or college is something else. They mark a real change in the graduate's life. Something important has happened, and it needs to be recognized. College and high school graduations bring the relatives out, hoisting their digital cameras.

Some of the high school graduates will still live with their parents and go to a local college or take their first jobs. For many it is a bigger change. They will go to college in a distant state. They will no longer be supported and supervised, fed and reminded to brush their teeth. They will be responsible for waking in the morning and doing their own laundry. Neither their life nor that of their family will ever be the same again.

For college graduates the change is even greater. They are about to leave the safe embrace of the family and go out into the real world. Even if they detour to graduate or professional school the plunge into reality is only postponed, not avoided. Before long they will live where everything counts, where nothing is forgiven, and where no excuses are accepted. They will be responsible for everything they are or do.

Our lives are always changing. There are no exceptions. For all of us aging begins at birth. Children grow up quickly. The young are soon middle aged. We grow older with each passing day, until one day we find to our surprise that we are indeed older.

Graduation is a beginning, not an end. We don't graduate from a school. We graduate into life.

# Good Intentions Can Go Very Wrong

Hawaii had a problem with rats. They ate the sugar cane that was an important crop in the islands. Someone had a brilliant idea: import some mongooses to eat the rats. They brought 72 mongooses from Jamaica.

It wasn't such a good idea after all. Rats are night animals, sleeping all day and coming out at night. The mongoose sleeps at night and eats all day. The two don't meet very often..

The result is that mongooses don't eat many rats. They eat other things. In fact, a mongoose will eat almost anything that doesn't eat it first. They particularly like bird's eggs, so they pretty well wiped out the birds on the islands. They also carried diseases as well as the rats did and they multiply like rabbits. Those 72 immigrants turned into a very big family.

The story of the Hawaiian mongoose is an example of good intentions going horribly wrong. They wanted to get rid of the rats. Instead they have as many rats as ever, some endangered birds are nearly extinct, and mongooses are spreading diseases all over the place.

Some people do bad things because they are bad people. Others do bad things without intending to. Good intentions don't make bad decisions better. A good person with bad judgment is just as dangerous as a bad person with good judgment.

With good intentions Americans once amended the constitution to make selling alcohol illegal. It was a bad solution to a bad problem. They aimed at sobriety, and got Al Capone and bad liquor. They meant well, but created new problems without solving the old one.

A British prime minister bargained with Hitler and announced he had bought "peace in our time." The peace was brief and Jews continued to die in the concentration camps. The prime minister was not a bad man. He was a good man who was disastrously wrong.

Almost everyone wants peace in the world. We all agree about that. We disagree about how to get it. Some ways of seeking peace make violence more likely.

Jesus told his disciples that being as gentle as doves is not enough. We must also be as wise as serpents.

# A Giraffe In Florence

What kind of gift will impress the man who has everything, someone like Bill Gates or Warren Buffet? Maybe a giraffe would work. It apparently did for the Sultan of Egypt.

The Sultan wanted to impress Lorenzo de Medici, the head of the first family of Florence in 1486. So he gave Lorenzo a giraffe, which was one thing he didn't already have. The trouble was that Lorenzo not only didn't have a giraffe, he didn't know what to do with the one the Sultan sent gave him. We've all had presents like that.

A historian surmises that "Crowds followed Lorenzo's giraffe" which "wandered along the city streets, raising its head to acknowledge admirers looking out from second story windows." After all, the Florentines had never seen a giraffe before.

But the giraffe had never seen an Italian looking out of a window before. The merchant looking out of the window was no more surprised than the beast looking in.

A giraffe in medieval Florence was like a rural minister in Las Vegas. The giraffe had never seen anything like it before, and wasn't sure he wanted to see it now. Merchants can adapt better than giraffes can.

We all have giraffe days, times when the world seems strange in ways we could never have expected. There was a time when even in their nightmares people didn't imagine schools needing on-site police officers or travelers having their shoes x-rayed. The National Geographic charmed us with pictures of beaming children in foreign lands. We didn't see them blasting away at each other with AK-47's. People responded to injustice by forming labor unions, not by planting roadside bombs or vaporizing themselves in crowded markets.

That doesn't mean that the world used to be a paradise. It had its own problems. The giraffe's Africa wasn't perfect either. Giraffes suffered in droughts and fell prey to lions there. But these were familiar horrors, not unthinkable ones.

Maybe we can get used to this strange new world. Or maybe we can't, or don't want to. Maybe we are paralyzed by fear of the unknown.

That depends on whether you're a merchant or a giraffe.

# A Sudden Change in Life

What do you do when the world falls apart? How can we go on when the veneer of civilization by which we live – the "thou shalts" and "thou shall nots" – crack open and the unthinkable must be thought?

It happens. A crazed youth on a college campus or a zealot strapped with explosives in Baghdad destroy the fragile certainties that make civilized life possible. The calculated cruelties of the concentration camp violate our confidence in humanity. Heartless genocide and unbridled terrorism break down the barriers that keep out chaos.

These events always raise questions we cannot answer. But there are a few questions we can answer, little patches of solid ground on which we can keep our footing.

The first is that there is no perfect defense against unmitigated evil. No law will restrain the lawless. No appeals to decency will deter those already outside decency's bounds. We can never be sure that we are safe, at any time, in any place.

There is good news however. In every shocking tragedy there are heroes as well as destroyers, and the heroes outnumber the destroyers. The elderly professor throws his body against the door so the students can escape. The fire fighter goes into the falling building without thinking of her personal cost. When events are determined by the worst in humanity, the best that was hidden comes out. In the end love rules: that love than which there is none greater. People do willingly lay down their lives for another.

Unimaginable tragedy forces us to decide who we are and what we want to be. It either drives us together or forces us apart. We either strike out fearfully at everyone around or reach comforting arms to all the others.

In terrible times we do not look for strength to the engineers or theologians. It is the poets and musicians who know the language of the unspeakable. Hymns say things that sermons cannot. The deep truths that save us are not found in a user's manual.

"… and when the fight is fierce, the warfare long
Steals on the ear the distant triumph song
And hearts are brave again, and arms are strong."

# Life Has Its Seasons

When the first snow falls some people move south to escape winter. Others stay where they are because they like seeing the seasons change. Both will probably get their wish.

In the Midwest we see the seasons change a lot. We can go from winter to summer and back to winter in an afternoon. It isn't only March that can come in like a lamb and leave like a lion. Lamb days and lion days can alternate any week of the year.

Some days we aren't sure what the season is. Only one thing is certain about a Midwestern season. It will change. Nothing lasts forever.

When we are young our hearts are easily broken. A bad grade in school or the break-up of a relationship or rejection by our peers can loom so large that we believe our life is ruined. It isn't. A bad day is only a day, and the sun will still rise tomorrow. When the worst has happened the best is still before us.

When bad things overtake us we are likely to ask all the wrong questions. We wonder why this happened to us or what we did to deserve it. There is only one right question to ask. It is "What should I do now?"

Our changing seasons are not the story of what life does to us. They are about what we do, in the best and the worst of times.

"It was the best of times, it was the worst of times." That is the beginning of Dickens novel "A Tale of Two Cities." The best and the worst are the beginning of the story, not the end. The winter of despair is never far from the spring of hope. Sometimes they are so close together that it is impossible to see one without the other.

Life has its seasons. There are sunny days and stormy ones, and both are only part of the story. There is another chapter we haven't seen yet. It is said that an opera isn't over until the fat lady sings. On the worst season of your life you can hear her warming up, but she hasn't started her song.

# Dysfunctional Families

The current fad in television is portraying dysfunctional families. The housewives are all desperate, the brothers and sisters lie to one another, and it's not clear who is the father. Every family has its obligatory homosexual, its despised bigot, and its weepy neurotic.

It wasn't always like that. Once television dads called out "I'm home, honey" as they came in the house, suited and necktied. Honey, not a hair out of place after a day of baking cakes and pies and making clothes for the entire family, beamed a smiling welcome. The children, all polite and obviously loved, waited for Dad to give sage advice for their minor problems.

It wasn't real, of course. Even the actors didn't have families like that. They were as likely as others in Hollywood to substitute serial polygamy for family life. Their children were already practicing for their tell-all books on the failures of their parenting.

The two pictures of family life are equally false. Real families don't communicate freely and comfortably. Parents commonly don't have any idea what teen-agers are thinking. Most adolescents go through a silent phase when they speak mainly in monosyllables.

On the other hand, the lack of communication doesn't always mean that dark secrets are being hidden. It doesn't even mean that everybody is talking and nobody is listening. I am frequently surprised at how much I remember that my parents said, even though at the time my only response was "Whatever."

Of course there are families that are shockingly bad and others that are very, very good. Both extremes are rare. Most families are neither as good as we hope nor as bad as we fear. Most have times of sheer joy and times that tear our hearts. In the end most families will be remembered for their happiness, not their struggles.

That we are entertained by accounts of disastrous families and not by impossibly good ones tells a lot about us but very little about family life. In that Ozzie and Harriet era we dreamed of what we wished our families were. Now we are encouraged by knowing that our families are a lot better than the ones on television.

# Another Universe Beyond This One

It is one thing to be in a winter storm in the Middle West. It is quite another thing to read about it on a nice day in Florida. You're bound to feel a little guilty about basking in the tropical sun while the hostages you left behind are coping with life in blizzard country. Like the rain, snow falls on the just and the unjust. Nobody deserves it.

Some bad things we bring on ourselves, and we should feel guilty. Some are done to us by other people, and they should be ashamed. Some just happen, they are nobody's fault, and nobody is guilty. They are part of living in this unruly world.

There is no sure connection between our blessings and our deeds. Everybody, good or bad, gets the same weather and suffers the same diseases. The best people sometimes die unrewarded and the worst may live to savor the harvest of their evil.

It isn't fair. Life is unfair.

One of the ironies of creation is that the human, the only creature to know the difference between right and wrong, is the one who must see the unfairness of life. We know what justice is, and we know that sometimes it comes too late.

Saints die unnoticed before their dreams are fulfilled. Bloody-handed dictators persist in their depredations. Many lives end as unfinished stories. We want to know the rest of the story.

The most important question we can ask is, "Is this all that there is?"

That same human, able to know good and evil, is able to conceive of good and evil too large to be completed in this universe. From the most primitive humans to those living now they have sought to see the invisible and expect universes beyond the one in which they lived. That is how they learned to pray.

We search for meaning in life. We want to know that it is better to reject temptations than to give in to them. We want to know that it is better to give than to take. We want to know that what we have is good now, but who we are is good forever.

# Children on a Trip

One child on a trip in a car is a responsibility. Two are a competition. Three or more are a traveling circus. Anyone who has traveled with children has heard two things a lot of times. The first is a question: "Are we there yet?" The second is a denial: "He (or she) started it."

No one can prod your weak spots like a sibling. Brothers and sisters know the words that hurt, and they don't hesitate to say them. What would start a fight between strangers is a normal squabble in a family.

When brothers or sisters quarrel, there is only one side others can safely take: the outside. No amount of childish teasing or adolescent abuse can change one thing. They care about one another. They will support one another against the world. To the question "Are you your brother's keeper?" they answer that of course they are. What hurts one hurts them all.

Family ties are intergenerational. Parents and grandparents, children and grandchildren are all in the family circle of caring. They rejoice at one another's joy and share their common suffering. They hope for one another, and reach out to one another.

There is an old hymn about the ties that bind us to people we love. One stanza notes that "often for each other flows the sympathizing tear." It takes a lot of tears to bind a family. We hope for the best in one another, pray for the moral victories of one another. In many families there are those for whom the others pray. We will do all we can for each other.

What they can't do is be one another. No matter how much we grieve for those we love, there is a limit to what we can do for them. In the end, all of us must make our own decisions, even bad ones, and pay the penalty for our own failures. The most important things are the ones we must do for ourselves. No family love, however deep, can change that.

The people we love most are often our greatest happiness. Sometimes they are our most painful sorrow. Either way, love never fails.

# We Can't Choose Our Gifts

Really good singers and dancers make their art look easy. Every movement seems natural and relaxed, every note seems unrehearsed. The years of training and the hours of practice are hidden from us. It almost seems that I could do it myself. The truth is that I can't.

Our life is partly the result of gifts we can't earn and partly of the effort we make to develop those gifts. What some can do well without much effort others must try very hard to do at all.

Training and perseverance could make me a better performer, but not a great one. At best I could learn a kind of acceptable mediocrity. We explain the difference by saying that the artist is gifted. That's partly true. Some people have talents the rest of us don't have.

We can't choose our gifts. God does that. We can't choose the part of the world our parents live in either. Some people have a better chance to use their gifts than others. A baby born in to parents in Chicago's south side has different opportunities than one whose home is in a wealthy north shore suburb. The accident of birth that caused both to be born in America has an even greater effect on their lives. That is a gift none of us earned and didn't choose.

It isn't just a matter of money. If the one baby has an alcoholic father and a thrice-divorced mother and the other is the child of an African American pastor and his loving wife the neighborhood won't make up for the difference. Parents are a gift, too.

Gifts and talent alone are not enough for greatness. Talent is the raw material from which greatness can be made. It can be developed or not. That depends not only on the person who has the gift but on other people who encourage or discourage it. Would we ever have heard of Tiger Woods if he had a different father?

The world doesn't give us equal opportunities. We can't choose our gifts. We can only be thankful and make the most of them. We can't all be American idols, but we can be useful.

# Doing Many Things Badly

My cell phone was the latest model, for a half hour or so after it was introduced. Progress in electronics means three things. Make the product smaller, make it do more things, or solve some problem in the last new version.

I'm glad that cell phones are smaller than the early ones. They had the size and shape of a paving block. But my new phone is so small that I don't know what pocket the phone is in. I have to slap myself like a man attacked by killer bees to answer an unexpected call.

We miss some calls because the cell phone isn't turned on. My new phone is always on, waiting to answer incoming calls. This creates a new problem. Airlines insist that I turn the phone off. The new phone solves this by creating an "airplane mode". This is turned on by going through several menus and selecting an option. That does the same thing as an off button.

There are other times when I don't want to be embarrassed by phone noises. I have to use airplane mode in church or at a Rotary meeting. I sometimes forget to do this in movie theaters. I have to stand up, slapping my pockets, while the phone shrieks "Yankee Doodle". This creates a certain amount of hostility.

My new phone will however take pictures. This illustrates the Swiss Army Knife theory of progress. With phones that are also cameras, music devices, and movie screens, can the combination chain saw and electric tooth brush be far behind? Like the Swiss Army Knife this phone will do a lot of things badly, but none of them very well. Exactly what can you cut with a tiny pair of scissors that will fold into a pocket knife?

The new and improved cell phone is matched by new and improved religion. Faith can be made smaller, serve more functions, and solve old problems. Short and snappy prayers get to the point quickly. Faith can make us healthy and wealthy as well as reverent. Fast paced action can solve the problem of boredom.

Maybe it would be real progress in faith to do one thing well.